"No tricks here, just a finely developed ear, a sure minded dramatic sense and passion hand-in-hand with compassion."
—Edward Albee

"Tom Donaghy is a young playwright who manges to understand the older generation while remaining a leading spokesman for his own. His plays are tender and lyrical: he has an acute eye and a sharp ear. He explores the everyday lives of ordinary Americans and makes them glow. His work is often moving and always beautiful."
—André Bishop

"Witty and bright and full of compassion for his characters, and by extension us. I think he likes people more than I do."
—Christopher Durang

"Donaghy possesses the rare gift of recognizing and describing the absolutely appropriate detail that suddenly makes clear huge portions of secret emotional life—in a moment, in a scene, in the description of a setting, in knowing what characters would force themselves to talk about when they are working furiously to avoid the life-and-death issues that are foremost in their minds. And it is this gift of detail that lifts his writing from the level of well-crafted storytelling to that of brilliant, contemporary, American art."
—Gerald Gutierrez

"Tom Donaghy's plays eschew the fashion for showing fangs. There is nothing postmodern about them, no high-flown wordplay, no satire, no social climbing masquerading as bitterness toward one's own family, no non-linear high jinks, no easy blame, no deliberate obscurity, no elitism. What these plays evince first and foremost is a respect and genuine affection without sentimentality—or its mirror image, cynicism—for working people and the real difficulties of lives being liv

TOM DONAGHY

# The Beginning of August and Other Plays

*The Dadshuttle*

*Northeast Local*

*Minutes from the Blue Route*

*The Beginning of August*

Grove Press
New York

*Published simultaneously in Canada*
*Printed in the United States of America*

FIRST EDITION

Library of Congress Cataloging-in-Publication Data

Donaghy, Tom.
     The beginning of August and other plays / Tom Donaghy.—1st ed.
        p. cm
     Contents: The dadshuttle—Northeast local—Minutes from the Blue Route—The beginning of August.
     ISBN 0-8021-3724-5
     I. Title.
     PS3554.O4643 B44 2000
     812'.54—dc21          00-032143

Grove Press
841 Broadway
New York, NY 10003

00 01 02 03   10 9 8 7 6 5 4 3 2 1

# CONTENTS

# ACKNOWLEDGMENTS

My thanks to everyone at each theater where the plays have been produced, especially those theaters where the plays have premiered. I need to single out for special thanks Toni Amicarella, Jennifer Kiger, Jerry Patch, Peter Manning, Tom Creamer, Susan Booth, Doug Hughes, Michael Wilson, André Bishop, Bernie Gersten, and Andrew Flatt who called 911. Of course I am grateful to everyone at Atlantic, from David and Bill to Emma and Buddy. I must also thank the actors, directors, and designers for their faith and community.

Thanks most especially to those who have made it easier for me to work, including—but not excluded to—my family (with Michael getting the purple heart); the Philly and Hofstra contingents with big love; Isaac, whose counsel has proved invaluable; Alec Mapa who told Kenn Russell who got on the phone to Grove; Kate Ryan, whose many generosities got me through many deprivations; Edward, who gave me a room in Montauk when I first started; Miranda and Charlotte; Marion Koltun Dienstag; Ian Falconer; Elizabeth Franz; Wendall Harrington; Geoff Stier; Matt McGrath; John Bruce; Ben Sprunger; Peter Gatiens; Debra Weinstein; and Joan whose various gifts of escape have always arrived with unerring timing. Mary and Neil should be thanked here as well for their incalculable support across the board. And the men of Olive, for their minds and their hearts and their timely rescue.

I must also thank my agents through the years, especially Sarah Jane Leigh, the intrepid. Finally, I extend special gratitude to the Guggenheim Foundation, the National Endowment for the Arts, the Berilla Kerr Foundation, PEN American, The MacDowell Colony, and Eric Price at Grove/Atlantic who has given me a great gift with this collection.

# THE DADSHUTTLE

for Michael, who dances instead

The *Dadshuttle* had its premiere at Atlantic Theater Company (Neil Pepe, Artistic Director; Jeffrey Solis, Managing Director) in New York City in February 1993. The play was directed by William H. Macy. The scenery was designed by James Wolk, the costumes by Sarah Edwards and the lighting by Howard Werner. The stage manager was Chris de Camillis. The cast was:

| | |
|---|---|
| **JUNIOR** | Matt McGrath |
| **SENIOR** | Peter Maloney |

The play takes place in a car en route to 30th Street Station, Philadelphia. It is late November, early evening.

*Lights up on* SENIOR *and* JUNIOR *in a car. Senior drives. Junior is in the passenger seat.*

**JUNIOR**    And why did they call him "Yank"?

**SENIOR**    Oh, you know, there's—when he was a kid he used to . . . I don't know, it was—

**JUNIOR**    They just called him that because he—

**SENIOR**    It was a name he got somewhere along the line. But, oh, he worked for them twenty-five, thirty years. Gets this frequent-flier pass—but I mean for the train. Now he just goes back and forth. Packs a bag. Doesn't talk to his kids.

**JUNIOR**    Why doesn't he talk to his kids?

**SENIOR**    He's like—that whole family is—nice kids too! They call him up. He just gets on the train. We don't pay too much attention to him. He used to come 'round.

**JUNIOR**    Does Mom-Mom see him?

**SENIOR**    Oh, you know, he calls every three months or so. Sees him at the funerals. Doesn't talk to his kids.

**JUNIOR**    Why doesn't he talk to his kids? He's just senile? That whole—

**SENIOR**    —that whole family! You know, your mother, she'd tell you the whole family—you know—they're crazy! *(beat)* You know, your Mom-Mom likes those cards you send her. I read them.

**JUNIOR**    Oh my God, they're so silly. You read them?

**SENIOR**    When I go over, sure.

**JUNIOR**    She keeps telling me to stop into church. *(laughing)* She wants me to be a priest.

5

**SENIOR**  Yeah, well, you know, she's goes to church and all. She's used to go up to the St. Patty's, when she went up. Light a candle. Some holy water. Get a hot dog. Take the train back. Just send her a little note now and then. Gives her something to do. Takes her mind off.

**JUNIOR**  Yeah, she wants me to be a priest. She can't quite figure it out.

**SENIOR**  Yeah, well. (*beat*) Joey's a priest up there.

**JUNIOR**  Yeah, she gave me his address. I don't think we'd have a lot—

**SENIOR**  —too much in common, no. He's a smart kid, though. They sent him over to Rome. Meet the Pope. He meets the Pope! He writes these articles. About saints and all.

**JUNIOR**  I guess she still sees me as an altar boy. It's my angelic face.

*Senior laughs.*

**JUNIOR** (*cont.*)  There's all that family I don't even know. You—all your cousins—

**SENIOR**  They were all around, in the house.

**JUNIOR**  You had, like, fifteen people! It was like this exercise in extended familial relations. Like, how far can we extend it.

**SENIOR**  Nah, not—well, we had Ray and Chuckie. Chuckie's kids, Dwayne and Eddie. Miriam and Timmy and their kids, Mike, Timmy, the others—after we lost little Ann Marie, five or six or so. Jimmy's friend Red . . . Kelly . . . Fat Bob. Dad—your grandfather—in the front room, your Mom-Mom, Bobby, Kevin, me. Your aunt Sal later.

6

Yeah, something like that. About fifteen. There were about fifteen, sure, I'd say. Maybe sixteen after Sal. She'd have her girlfriends over too, 'fore she married Mack. Was pretty full.

**JUNIOR**   And this was a *row house*?

**SENIOR**   Twin. Connected to Ray's place.

**JUNIOR**   Right. (*beat*) Uncle Mack still drinking?

**SENIOR**   Oh, we haven't seen them since the reunion.

**JUNIOR**   I never understood why families have picnics on battlefields.

**SENIOR**   Huh.

**JUNIOR**   It just strikes me odd. All this Frisbee throwing on top of mass gravesites.

**SENIOR**   Yeah, well. Everybody has a good time. They like to see each other.

**JUNIOR**   It's just odd.

**SENIOR**   That's Philly. All those old places. Keeps your mother busy. She likes to watch them make candles.

**JUNIOR**   She makes candles?

**SENIOR**   Yeah. No—your mother? No. Those people dressed like colonial times. At the Gettysburg. In Lincoln's house. Gets her away from your Mom-Mom.

**JUNIOR**   How's Dr. Merrick going?

**SENIOR**   Good. Seems good. Your mother likes it. Well, you two talk.

**JUNIOR**   Seems happy with it. But, you know, we don't talk about everything. She's funny. She keeps using phrases like "growth potential" and "emotionally responsible." She says—

**SENIOR**   Yeah, well.

**JUNIOR**   (*beat*) Marty doesn't like it, though?

**SENIOR**   Oh, he's just—he just got upset 'cause no one told him and he thought it was some big secret or something. You know, out here no one—he doesn't know any people who do that. I mean, when we—we didn't—

**JUNIOR**   There've got to be people in Drexel Hill who're in therapy. I mean, it's a truly troubled town.

**SENIOR**   Well, you know, he wondered why she wouldn't talk to *us* about whatever it was . . . that was . . . bothering her, you know?

**JUNIOR**   But he doesn't talk to anyone at home anyway.

**SENIOR**   It's this phase. You all went through it. He takes everything too serious. He's got all that acne. You all went through it.

**JUNIOR**   He's like her.

**SENIOR**   He's like your mother alright. I always said none of you ever had a finger of me. (*beat*) Put the roof on that building.

**JUNIOR**   That there? Looks like the Chrysler Building?

**SENIOR**   Yeah, put the roof on it. Back some time ago.

**JUNIOR**   You still don't go up on those things?

**SENIOR**  Nah, let the younger guys do that. Sometimes I go up. They threw this guy off last month. The Teamsters threw this guy off.

**JUNIOR**  Off the ROOF?

**SENIOR**  Yeah, he wasn't—he was gypping them out of something or other. Never got the whole story.

**JUNIOR**  Oh, my God, what happened?

**SENIOR**  Nothing. No one admitted it. They all wanted him out of the way, so forth.

**JUNIOR**  No one was charged?

**SENIOR**  Nah, they just threw him off.

**JUNIOR**  They do that?

**SENIOR**  Sure. Not all the time. That's not business as scheduled. No one said anything, you know. But, you know, sure, even if you aren't getting thrown off, you could still fall off. Some guys have fallen off.

**JUNIOR** (*beat*)  Paul's father does that too.

**SENIOR**  Huh.

**JUNIOR**  You remember my friend. Paul.

**SENIOR**  Yeah, your friend we met outside the dorm?

**JUNIOR**  Yeah.

**SENIOR**  That's not that waiter spilled that drink on your mother's coat?

**JUNIOR**  No, God, that was some kid from school. You met him outside the dorm. Paul. You met him when—

**SENIOR**  Yeah, sure.

9

**JUNIOR** (*beat*)  His father does what you do.

**SENIOR**  Huh.

**JUNIOR**  I don't really know what you do, though. When people ask me, all I know is you go to lunch a lot.

**SENIOR**  Yeah, well, I do a lot of that. That's why I'm in demand. There's these young guys don't know how to talk to people. These contractors, they know me from way back, these guys. We go out. We went to this great place the other day. Boy oh boy, they had lobsters the size a—boy, I ate too much or something. Then your mother gets mad when I don't eat a big dinner, so forth.

**JUNIOR**  I didn't think she had time to cook anymore.

**SENIOR**  That's what Marty says. He says the guy at the pizza place thinks he's an orphan, and Marty keeps asking your mother who she is and all. I mean, I don't know what he wants her to cook. He eats pizza, he eats sandwiches, nothing else, you know.

**JUNIOR**  He's so odd. He's never eaten spaghetti.

**SENIOR**  He says—what's he say? Yeah—he "objects to the texture." He's getting better, you know. He's got all these friends coming to the house now. Big kids. They come in the house.

**JUNIOR**  Girlfriend?

**SENIOR**  There's this one girl calls him up. We kid him about it. He never calls her though. She always calls.

**JUNIOR**  (*beat*)  Penny says hi.

**SENIOR**  Huh. What's she up to?

**JUNIOR**   Being an actress, like everyone else. I don't see her usually. She was catering this thing at this club and I saw her. And she's getting married. Maybe.

**SENIOR**   Huh. (*beat*) Yeah, your mother likes those colonial things.

**JUNIOR** (*beat*)   There was this performance artist at the club.

**SENIOR**   Yeah? What's that?

**JUNIOR**   Oh, kind of an avant-garde, one-person-show-type things.

**SENIOR**   Like that play we saw with that Jean-Claude guy with all the scarves?

**JUNIOR**   Yeah! Kind of like that. She's—she's—she does this weird thing, this show, and she sprays herself all over with different . . . it's kind of—

**SENIOR**   Huh.

**JUNIOR**   It's kind of funny. She's pretty well known—up there.

**SENIOR**   Huh. She get paid for that?

**JUNIOR**   Oh, yeah, sure. Not much, you know. It's not like a TV show. It's—sure—she'll come to your parties and—well, she wouldn't come to *your* parties—but, you know, she has an incredible following and—

**SENIOR**   Yeah, Stevie's kid got christened last week.

**JUNIOR** (*beat*)   God, she's been pregnant forever.

**SENIOR**   Oh, yeah, sure—no, this is the second one.

**JUNIOR**   What? Isn't Stevie my age?

**SENIOR**  Yeah, your age. (*beat*) They had this party afterwards and they had all those vegetable things your mother likes. They had a spinach . . . in a loaf of bread.

**JUNIOR**  Huh. What does Stevie do?

**SENIOR**  Oh, he's—

**JUNIOR**  When he's not breeding.

**SENIOR**  Something or other. They just bought a house. 'Round Mary's way.

**JUNIOR**  We gonna make this train?

**SENIOR**  Sure, we're hitting all the lights here. (*beat*) How's the apartment?

**JUNIOR**  Fine. Good. Alright. You know.

**SENIOR**  How's the job?

**JUNIOR**  Okay. How's work?

**SENIOR**  Good, good. You know, it's—it's—

**JUNIOR**  Yeah. (*beat*) I wanted to—

**SENIOR**  Can't sleep past five anymore.

**JUNIOR**  Yeah, I can't believe you drive all the way to Delaware. I wanted to ask—

**SENIOR**  Your mother gets mad when I fall asleep early.

**JUNIOR**  Yeah. I wanted to ask, when I—if I, when I come home—

**SENIOR**  Uh-huh.

**JUNIOR**  When I come home for Christmas? If someone—I could bring someone?

SENIOR   Oh, you have to ask your mother about those things. She's, you know, COOKING, we're running around, she's worrying, we have to visit people, she's worried—with the cakes, the kids, Sally's kids over—

JUNIOR   I'd like to have Paul over. He's—

SENIOR   You know, the TREE—

JUNIOR   Paul.

SENIOR   That waiter friend?

JUNIOR   No. He's not the waiter. I mean, he is *a* waiter. I just thought it might be—have him—

SENIOR   Your mother handles those things.

JUNIOR   His parents—

SENIOR   Where's his parents?

JUNIOR   They're at home. At his house. I just thought it would be nice.

SENIOR   You know, the breakfast. (*beat*) What does his father do?

JUNIOR   (*beat*)   He does what you do?

SENIOR   Huh. (*beat*) Your mother had me over to the Edgar Allan Poe house last week. Just a house. I mean, it's not even the real house. They just built this replica.

JUNIOR   You think she'd say yes?

SENIOR   He didn't even write anything there, he just lived there and his wife had tuberculosis or something there. They show you this place on the third floor where she spit up blood.

**JUNIOR**  You know, it'd only be for two days.

**SENIOR**  Sure, sure. We got Madeleine's house to visit. She'll make that special vegetarian dish for you.

**JUNIOR**  I'm not a vegetarian! It's just—I'm not. A vegetarian. I just don't eat red meat. Everyone keeps saying I'm—it's funny. I eat fish and chicken. So I'm not really a hard and fast—then they look real disappointed when I tell them I'm not—

**SENIOR**  You still work in that bar?

**JUNIOR**  What? Oh. It's not really a bar. It's more like a . . . club. No, that was for the summer.

**SENIOR**  Yeah, we're still reading about all this stuff.

**JUNIOR**  Nah, I don't work there anymore.

**SENIOR**  For years now this stuff, this stuff in the magazines. We picked up *Newsweek* last week at the, uh—

**JUNIOR**  It was just a temporary job.

**SENIOR**  —the, uh, Wawa. *Time*—*People* magazine keeps having these articles. All these young guys in New York City—

**JUNIOR**  I work in an office now.

**SENIOR**  Girls now too.

**JUNIOR**  It's pretty easy. I just sit behind a desk.

**SENIOR**  These young people get sick. They don't get better. They don't have enough beds. They put them in with the Puerto Ricans, drug addicts—they only have a few beds.

**JUNIOR**  It's not as bad as that.

**SENIOR**  And then they go to their families—their families—and they spend all kinda money because—

**JUNIOR**  I take care of myself.

**SENIOR**  It's costly, you know, insurance companies are, they're saying—it just seems horrible, all that—

**JUNIOR**  Listen.

**SENIOR**  —all that sickness. When you get sick you can't do anything and they give them this test—

**JUNIOR**  Listen to me, listen, okay?

**SENIOR**  —and no one's ever—they still don't have anything they can give you, you just get sicker—

**JUNIOR**  I don't have sex I don't have sex I haven't had sex in a while!

**SENIOR**  *(beat)*  Your mother bought this Cape Cod bench for the porch. I was out painting it last Saturday.

**JUNIOR**  You hear me?

**SENIOR**  Then she wants me to paint the trim to go with the bench. The . . . not the trim, the uh . . .

**JUNIOR**  I won't get sick.

**SENIOR**  The, uh, the . . . railing there. The gate thing. And then she doesn't like the color of the gate. So I have to paint it this "burnt amber" she picked out of that pamphlet. Next Friday after work. In the garage. You still want that cabinet?

**JUNIOR**  No. It's too big. It doesn't fit in the . . .

**SENIOR**  We'll keep it for Marty—

JUNIOR   —Keep it for Marty. (*beat*) Mommy show you all those pictures she found? The ones with the polka-dot shirts?

SENIOR   Nah.

JUNIOR   All of us in the backyard? In the polka-dot shirts? Peter's about two. There's a picture of the four of us in those polka-dot shirts. You know the ones. The ones I used to hide from you when you wore them to Baker's. The clown shirts you had. The ones the salesgirls laughed at.

SENIOR   Oh, yeah, sure. Had about ten of them.

JUNIOR   You used to wear them when we went down Margate. On the boardwalk. We'd go up and get some Copper Kettle fudge and you'd return it and tell them someone must've thrown something in one of the vats! Must be a bad batch—

SENIOR   —Bad batch!

JUNIOR   Talking at the top of your voice! With those polka-dot—and those big sandals. Like some gladiator clown. I was so mortified. You were this giant loud person.

SENIOR   Still am.

JUNIOR   In restaurants when you'd hit the glass with your fork to get the waitress? And then flirt with her while Mommy giggled. I wanted to throw myself in the ocean! (*beat*) We're all in the backyard. In the pictures. We wouldn't wear them in public. But, you know, in the backyard it was okay, you know, in those shirts it was . . . all that fabric, it was like—all that fabric on our little bony bodies.

SENIOR   Yeah, sure. She just find them?

JUNIOR   Yeah, she found them.

**SENIOR**  Those Polaroids. Huh.

**JUNIOR**  Yeah, they were in a box.

**SENIOR**  Oh, you know, those boxes! All alphabetical in the attic. She takes them out. I look through.

**JUNIOR**  Uh-huh.

**SENIOR**  Look through just to see—we always said we'd take more pictures. There's a whole bunch of you and hardly any—

**JUNIOR**  —any of Marty, I know. Dad?

**SENIOR**  Good-looking kids.

**JUNIOR**  Daddy?

**SENIOR**  What, boy?

**JUNIOR**  (*beat*) Paul's sick. My friend Paul? He's sick.

**SENIOR**  Your waiter friend?

**JUNIOR**  Um . . .

**SENIOR**  Your mother find those Ocean City pictures?

**JUNIOR**  He wasn't feeling good all summer, he was fine, he kept saying, but he wasn't good.

**SENIOR**  Haven't seen those pictures in—

**JUNIOR**  He wasn't good. And the bed was soaked every night.

**SENIOR**  It's cold season. You gotta—it's fiber. And C, you know.

**JUNIOR**  Uh-huh.

**SENIOR**  B–complex. Mark's kids always have something. Come down with—they don't eat right.

**JUNIOR**  We finally, he was really sick one day and he went, and they gave him, they tested him for all kinds of things, and he came back home and—

**SENIOR**  You might miss your train. Bottleneck up ahead.

**JUNIOR**  But they told us the one test was positive—

**SENIOR**  Should've taken City Line.

**JUNIOR**  It was positive. Positive.

**SENIOR**  Always do this. (*beat*) Positive's good, isn't it?

**JUNIOR**  It means—no. It's not good. It's positive that it's there—whatever it is they're looking for. It's a . . . positive . . . it means . . .

**SENIOR**  (*simultaneous with Junior's next line*) . . . Yeah, we'll be heading up to the Roosevelt house next week . . . your mother wants to see Hyde Park . . . there's an exhibit she read about in the Weekend Section . . .

**JUNIOR**  . . . it's a negative thing but they call it positive, 'cause that's the terminology, if it came out negative it would be a positive thing, but, you know, it wasn't. It wasn't positive in that sense. And he always did all the right things like they've been telling us, but sometimes, when he first . . . but he's home now. And you'd never know except when he coughs, which he does every now and then. And he gets his T-shirts wet a lot so we got him a whole bunch at this flea market the other day for a dollar-something.

**SENIOR**  Uh-huh. (*beat*) Then we thought we'd head down to Penn State. See your brother.

**JUNIOR** And I feel fine and everything. I feel fine, you know, but they asked me if I'd like to check, just to check, just to maybe—and I said, "Sure." I hadn't, you know, I didn't need to, you know, worry. We'd been, always been doing what they'd, you know . . . it was just this little check and—

**SENIOR** Uh-huh.

**JUNIOR** I was kinda suprised that they suggested to even, you know, but it doesn't strike me as odd anymore if it, well—

**SENIOR** Huh.

**JUNIOR** I think about evolution. It's evolution and I *feel* fine. I mean, I feel that I *think* I'm fine. I look fine.

**SENIOR** You know.

**JUNIOR** I feel fine.

**SENIOR** Your mother.

**JUNIOR** You know, you know, and some people never get it.

**SENIOR** She took me.

**JUNIOR** They just carry it. They don't get it.

**SENIOR** She took me to.

**JUNIOR** They just, they don't get it. The whole thing.

**SENIOR** The Betsy Ross house. Drags me. All those places.

**JUNIOR** They stay healthy. Diet or acupuncture—whatever.

**SENIOR** All those places.

**JUNIOR** There are some things that I read about. I did read. I don't read anymore.

**SENIOR**   In the Betsy Ross house they have little stairs.

**JUNIOR** (*beat*)   Boy, that performance piece the other night, I'll tell you.

**SENIOR**   They preserve these houses. But they never fix the stairs. Because people were smaller then. You have to walk up . . . these . . . little . . . stairs. Because if you lived then. If you lived then. You were much . . . smaller.

*Senior cries.*

**JUNIOR** (*beat*)   I really appreciate you driving me. You know, I just hate the bus. See all those people from high school. So complacent. And fat. And bald. They never—they never GO anyplace! They think *here's*—you know? New York! New York—I just love it.

**SENIOR**   You know, I don't know what I'm gonna do with your mother. She used to be so much better, I thought. And then it just, before I knew it, she wasn't sleeping and then she—all this STUFF! You both like to talk about this stuff. There's so much more to talk about! Why do you talk about ALL THIS STUFF?

**JUNIOR**   Oh. I don't know. You know, it's just—we talk. She's, she'll be alright, you know . . .

**SENIOR**   Okay, okay.

**JUNIOR**   She'll be—it's—don't . . . please. I don't—please.

*They arrive at their destination.*

**SENIOR**   Okay. I'm okay. Okay. (*beat*) Pull around the side?

**JUNIOR**   Huh?

**SENIOR**   Pull around the—

**JUNIOR**   Oh. No. Here's fine. This is okay—right—here.

**SENIOR**   Here? Or over—

**JUNIOR**   No, here, I can walk to the, uh—stop. This is fine.

**SENIOR**   Okay, here you go. (*He puts the car in park.*) You need anything, you know—

**JUNIOR**   No.

**SENIOR**   We're fine. We're okay.

**JUNIOR**   Okay.

**SENIOR**   Call—

**JUNIOR**   Yeah, sure.

**SENIOR**   —your mother. Whenever. Here's something.

*Senior offers Junior some cash.*

**JUNIOR**   Thanks, I don't—

**SENIOR**   Milk shakes—

**JUNIOR**   —need this.

**SENIOR**   —or T-shirts. You know. Something. You know, or—

**JUNIOR**   Thanks. (*beat*) Thanks.

**SENIOR**   Take care, boy.

**JUNIOR**   Yeah, you too. Take care. I will—you—thanks. (*beat*) Okay. Okay. (*Junior reaches into the backseat for his bag.*) I've got it.

**SENIOR**   You got it?

**JUNIOR**   Yeah, it's a carry-on thing. Tell Marty I'm sorry I missed him.

**SENIOR**    Will do. He'll be sorry he—you—

**JUNIOR**    Take care. I will. You too, Daddy. I—Dad? Daddy?

**SENIOR**    What, boy?

**JUNIOR**    (*beat*)    You too.


*Lights fade. End of Play.*

# NORTHEAST LOCAL

for my dear Anna Mae, who thinks this is a very good play

"Who built the Seven Gates of Thebes?
The books are filled with names of kings.
Was it kings who hauled the craggy blocks of stones?"

—*A Worker Reads History*

Bertolt Brecht

*Northeast Local* was produced by Lincoln Center Theater (André Bishop, Artistic Director; Bernard Gersten, Executive Producer) at the Mitzi E. Newhouse Theater in New York City in October 1995. The play was directed by Gerald Gutierrez. The set was designed by John Lee Beaty, the costumes by Jane Greenwood, the lights by Brian MacDevitt, the sound by Otts Munderloh and the original music by Louis Rosen. The stage manager was Marjorie Horne. The cast was:

| | |
|---|---|
| **GI** | Mary Elizabeth Mastrantonio |
| **MICKEY** | Anthony LaPaglia |
| **MAIR** | Eileen Heckart |
| **JESSE** | Terry Alexander |

The play takes place over the course of thirty years. The set should suggest a rented room; Mair's parlor; a bar; a home for the elderly; a city apartment; and Gi and Mickey's living room, kitchen, dining room, upstairs hallway and front yard.

*Northeast Local* was originally produced by Trinity Repertory Company (Richard Jenkins, Artistic Director) in 1996. The play was directed by David Petrarca. The scenery was designed by Linda Buchanan; the costumes by William Lane; the lighting by James F. Ingalls; and the music and sound by Rob Milburn. The Stage Manager was Thomas Kauffman. The cast was:

| | |
|---|---|
| **GI** | Rengin Altay |
| **MICKEY** | Ed Shea |
| **MAIR** | Jane MacIver |
| **JESSE** | Allen Oliver |

# ACT ONE

*Late August, 1963. Morning. A rented room in a seaside community.*
*The surf is heard outside. A strong afternoon light comes in the*
*window.* MICKEY *and* GI, *both in their twenties, are in bed lying*
*naked under a white sheet. He is 25 and Irish-American. She is 23*
*and Italian-American.*

**MICKEY**    And I figure the kid's about three, four, years old
tops, right? Couldn'ta been more than five. 'Cause after five
they get, you know, formed in a certain way. Get minds,
opinions, what have you. Start catching on and look out! So
little dimply kid. Shirt and suspenders.

**GI**    A jumper?

**MICKEY**    No, like a German thing.

**GI**    Uh . . . ?

**MICKEY**    Germans wear them.

**GI**    A uniform?

**MICKEY**    Like them German dancers in the beer halls. Christ,
that Bavarian—

**GI**    Liederhosen?

**MICKEY**    Right! Like on those cuckoo clocks. Kid's got on a
liederhosen, puffy sleeves, kneesocks.

**GI**    Dear.

**MICKEY**    Whole kid picture. Patent-leather shoes.

**GI**    God!

**MICKEY**  Whole kid thing. And I just pick him up. Could just about scoop him up in my one arm and go, went, "Kid, you got the whole world in your future." 'Cause you wanna lie to kids. Right? Something about the way they trust you with those eyes. You know, so I go, "Kid—whole world in your future." Big lie. And kid goes back to me, just as loud as can be, loud as all get-out, "Uncle Mick, you got the whole world . . . up your fat behind."

**GI**  No!

**MICKEY**  Couldn'ta been more than two years old.

**GI**  Two years old!

**MICKEY**  Whole church turned around—and this is my father's funeral. Supposed to be on kid-muzzle duty and kid's screaming just as loud as holy hell that my behind's more round than a person's oughta be in his midget opinion. 'Course I was fifteen pounds heavier at the time. Can't tell now.

**GI**  No.

**MICKEY**  'Cause into more of a physical way of life.

**GI**  Well, it . . . shows. (*beat*) Hate church, all those kids screaming.

**MICKEY**  Screaming 'cause they wanna be outside! Rolling around on the lawn, kicking the crap outta each other, whatnot. (*beat*) You got the blackest hair.

**GI**  Yeah. (*beat*) My family's got a ton of kids too. Just thousands it seems, during Christmas—

**MICKEY**  Right?

30

**GI**  Christmas madhouse! Every holiday you got 'em over, screaming, crawling all over. Doing, you know, stuff in their pants. But being the youngest and all, of my family and all, the pressure's off a bit. To have kids—the pressure's off. Which is great and all 'cause I'm intending to do things and having kids right away can keep you from the world, so—

**MICKEY**  Oh, but kids—

**GI**  Oh, my God, kids, sure! But lotsa things to do. Plans. Not *specific* plans yet. Just kinda I know there're things out there that're gonna find me to do them is all. And figure there's time, got time.

**MICKEY**  Sure, but kids!

**GI**  Kids, sure, eventually—but I'm only twenty-three. And figure there's 'bout a million things I could do, you know, excel at, that should occur to me in the next two to three years. Twenty-five and I'll know. Two to three years and I know I'll know.

**MICKEY**  That puts me at the time-to-know range.

**GI**  But see, you know—you weld.

**MICKEY**  S'what I do.

**GI**  You're a big, capable welder.

**MICKEY**  S'what I am!

**GI**  But see most guys your age they're still doing—

**MICKEY**  What I *was* doing.

**GI**  Right, they're having fun.

**MICKEY**  Drinking! Hoho!

**GI**   They're drinking.

**MICKEY**   Hoho!

**GI**   They're having fun—

**MICKEY**   Sowing their wild—

**GI**   Sowing their wild—you know. Just this feeling I got. And thinking about stuff like I do. Always usually been right about them type of feelings. Least nearby to being right most times about stuff. Maybe I could possibly make speeches! I'm real good at communicating. My forensics teacher in high school said I had the ability to communicate with many people if I want to and that would be a thing I'd like to think about wanting to do. 'Cause I'd like a lot of people around me all the time. So to communicate with so many people by a speech or, right, like something I'd write or build or paint would be the best thing ever! And women today are getting lotta options and taking charge in ways— look at what she did with the White House, right?

**MICKEY**   'Cause she married a Catholic.

**GI**   No! But someday all different kindsa people are gonna surround me—not too close 'cause I'm a little claustrophobic. Something I'm working on.

**MICKEY**   You got the blackest hair I've ever seen.

**GI**   You keep saying.

**MICKEY**   That real?

**GI**   Oh.

**MICKEY**   'Cause it's so black.

**GI**   Um, it's real.

**MICKEY**   Don't look real.

**GI**   It's not that black.

**MICKEY**   Not that it looks *unreal*. It's just so real-looking it almost looks fake.

**GI**   Fake! (*she laughs*)

**MICKEY**   Don't mean that bad, fake bad. Mean fake in a good way.

**GI**   It's real, Mick.

**MICKEY**   Like fake in a real way. 'Cause it's *pretty* fake-looking if it isn't real.

**GI**   Yeah, no. Thanks. (*beat*) I'm gonna put my top on. (*finding it next to the bed, she puts it on*) It's nothing, just I'm having hot skin from the sun, then it's cold then it's hot again, so it's confusing. It's good here under the covers.

**MICKEY**   Nights at the beach get cold and then days real hot—who knows?

**GI**   I don't.

**MICKEY** (*beat*)   Gi.

**GI**   What?

**MICKEY**   It's pretty. When you say it. Gi. Your name. Gi.

**GI** (*beat*)   Better get dressed or I'll miss my train.

**MICKEY**   Trains leave the beach all the time.

**GI**   No, sure, it's just—

**MICKEY**   You got the express every hour.

**GI**   No, right, I know, but—

**MICKEY**   You hop on that, you'll be home no time.

**GI**   Yeah no, it's just—

**MICKEY**   What?

**GI**   It's just—"Gi" ain't my real name.

**MICKEY**   Huh?

**GI**   They just call me Gi 'cause it's just like a really quicker way to say Gina Maria Allegra. Even quicker than Gi-na. That's silly. But it's not so Italian when you cut it real short and just say "Gi."

**MICKEY**   More like French or something.

**GI**   Yeah?

**MICKEY**   Like *Gigi*. That movie with all those French people. That's what I thought it was from.

**GI**   No, it's from my aunt.

*He starts to kiss her all over.*

**GI** (*cont.*)   Her name's really Regina, really. Huh. I always thought it sounded French too. Maybe you're the only other person in the world who thinks that. (*beat*) I don't want to take the express train. 'Cause it just goes too fast for me. The local one stops at all these little towns, which is nice, little houses, all those little lives going on inside.

**MICKEY**   Could always hop the bus.

**GI**   No, buses smell funny.

**MICKEY**   Not if you sit in the front.

**GI**   But they're for poor people.

**MICKEY**   S'what we are.

**GI**   No we aren't, we're . . . practically strangers . . . (*She returns his kisses, then pulls away.*) Mick?

**MICKEY**   What?

**GI**   You can't say this though to anyone.

**MICKEY**   What?

**GI**   And you gotta swear 'cause it's a particular thing I have about letting this be known.

**MICKEY**   Swear.

**GI**   Which is something I don't want.

**MICKEY**   I'm swearing.

**GI**   I dye my hair.

*He holds her.*

**GI** (*cont.*)   It's all silver underneath. They called me names at home until I fixed it. Awful names. Was all silver. Just like an old lady's. And I'm 'bout the farthest thing from an old lady as I can get. Ain't I? I feel just about like just about the farthest thing from an old lady as I can just about get.

*Mickey's mother, MAIR, appears onstage. She is sixty years old and an Irish immigrant. Gi and Mickey get dressed in their Sunday best and visit her in her parlor. It is two months later.*

**MAIR**   Completely gray since I was twenty. And prouda it. 'Cause somethun's gotta give when you're running a household. Came over on that boat, two sisters dead, days on end, got to this street, married Carey, had the kids, first thing I did? Didn't dye the hair back red—

**MICKEY**   Boy, oh boy.

**MAIR** Stocked up the basement! Gotta keep a stocked basement full of canned goods, green beans, whatnot! Otherwise, you're in for trouble. 'Cause we came over with nothing, threw what we could in a little bag—

**MICKEY** You know, Mair—

**MAIR** Show her the bag.

**MICKEY** It's just a little—

**MAIR** C'mon, right next to the—

**MICKEY** Mair keeps the bag by the door.

**MAIR** Never know when the roof's gonna fall down around your ankles and then whatcha gonna do? If you don't got a stocked basement—potatoes, cabbage, green beans—and something to carry the necessities in, you got a whole lotta nothing. (*beat*) Found a commemorative plate in the basement from the assassination. You want that, Gi?

**GI** No, thanks.

**MAIR** Shame, him being Catholic and all.

**GI** So young to be a widow.

**MAIR** Well, we all get something to bear. (*to Mickey*) Glad you finally brought her 'round.

**MICKEY** Only been married two months.

**GI** Been meaning to get over since—

**MAIR** You know, colored folks love green beans. What makes them stay so young-looking. That Harry Belafonte?—he's fifty-five. Don't look a day over thirty.

**GI** Don't know if there's any connection between that and string beans.

36

**MICKEY**   You taking your heart medicine, Mair?

**MAIR**   Aww.

**GI**   Seems to me—in a can especially. How're you to even know there's any vitamins left? And right and it's the, um, vitamins that you'd think'd keep people's skin so young. But 'course I eat lots of string beans and I'm not black so don't see any—

**MICKEY**   Who knows, right?

**GI**   Don't believe there's any connection. (*beat*) Or even vitamins in canned things if there was to be a connection.

**MICKEY**   Gi gets fresh ones from the A&P.

**MAIR**   Huh.

**MICKEY**   And they taste like I don't know what! Like nothin' I ever tasted.

**MAIR**   Bet they're real fresh and all.

**MICKEY**   Just as fresh as I don't know what. And she steams them to keep in the vitamins.

**MAIR**   Molly, my youngest, had green beans at her wedding—huge wedding. Carey still alive, paid the whole thing—the hall, the flowers, lotsa rice. Your parents didn't wanna big wedding, guess, why you two did it at the City Hall?

**MICKEY**   Gi and I didn't—

**GI**   Getting into all that, it's so—

**MICKEY**   Her mother passed away last—

**GI**   And Dad's in Italy so—

MICKEY   Her father's in Italy!

MAIR   Well, that's far away.

GI (*beat*)   We have a sweet black couple just moved in down the block, sweetest souls, just really nice—

MICKEY   Can you imagine—Italy!

GI   They brought us a bread pudding, right and—first day there! And really a good one, not, you know, not a store-bought one. You could tell. So we heated it up.

MICKEY   Just got the new stove.

GI   So we heated it right up.

MICKEY   Self-cleaning!

MAIR   Mm.

MICKEY   You know, they say that, but at a certain point Gi finds herself on her hands and knees with gloves, a brush, and oven cleaner. You know, they say in the ad, "self-cleaning."

GI   Only to an extent.

MICKEY   To an extent it cleans itself, sure. But you just know the thing's not going to clean itself through and through.

GI   Ends up being me myself who's cleaning the self-cleaning oven!

MAIR (*beat*)   Maybe that's where they get the name. Maybe ain't worth the money Mickey put into it.

GI   Was a gift from my brother actually, his wife—

MAIR   Yeah, well, those colored people know how to cook things.

**GI** (*beat*)   You'll have to come over and see the house. I mean it looks like any other house.

**MICKEY**   Nah, it's not—

**GI**   Any other house for miles.

**MICKEY**   That price, sure.

**GI**   They all got the same shutters, roofs.

**MICKEY**   It's a boom.

**GI**   Same porches.

**MICKEY**   It's a building boom, and right down from my plant.

**GI**   We almost moved into the wrong one! Imagine.

**MAIR**   Huh.

**MICKEY**   So first thing I did? Planted two rhododendrons, right out front. One's named Mickey, one's named Gi. So, okay, they won't bloom till spring—

**MAIR**   What could Molly be doing is all I'm thinking! Invited the whole lot of 'em over—

**MICKEY**   Take a load off, Mair.

*Mair turns on her police radio.*

**MAIR**   Must be a roadblock, tree fell, some such thing.

**MICKEY**   Sure, this time, Sunday and all, the traffic. Everyone's trying to get out to see family, what have you.

**GI**   It's a family day and you being Mick's mother we wanted to—

**MAIR**   Could be some kinda emergency situation, something.

**MICKEY**   Mair, you remember Kid Mingey—?

**MAIR** You know, you get an ambulance in the road and's just all over. And this is the season, telling you. Winter comes, old folks line up to pass on. Sirens keep me up nights. Don't read the obituary page, just turn on my radio, listen to God take away half the people on Lancaster Avenue.

**MICKEY** Mair? Kid Mingey?

**MAIR** God's gotta piece of the action up the funeral home, let me tell you.

**MICKEY** Mingeys from Callaghan?

**MAIR** I hear ya.

**MICKEY** He remembers you.

**MAIR** Yeah, well, I make an impression. Apparently not on my other kids.

**MICKEY** What, me and Gi don't count?

**MAIR** You want some root beer?

**MICKEY** Nothing stronger?

**GI** We're fine.

**MAIR** And just root beer, s'all I'm offering.

**MICKEY** Mair, siddown.

**MAIR** You want it, you're just not saying it.

*Mair exits to kitchen.*

**MICKEY** Just an old lady.

**MAIR** (*off*) We talked about this shelf in here. When you were over last. I don't know a hammer from a—look at this—hanging by a screw! Could wait till hell freezes over, my kitchen'll be down around my ankles. I'll be standing in rubble!

**MICKEY**  She's just an old—

**MAIR**  (*off*)  Just hanging BY A SCREW!

**MICKEY**  (*calling to her*)  I'll come 'round one day this week.

**MAIR**  (*off*)  I'll make sure and hold my breath.

**MICKEY**  (*to Gi*)  I'll pull the car around so it's right there.

**GI**  Mick, you gotta be here!

**MICKEY**  Two minutes. I'll pull it right around.

*He dashes out. After a moment, Mair reenters carrying a tray of root beer and cookies.*

**MAIR**  You know if you don't attend things they just end up getting unattended to and then jars are falling and I could cut myself again like last time with that awful cheese-slicer thing, that gizmo Bud got me for Christmas. What am I doing with a cheese slicer? Tried to use it on a peach, almost lost a thumb. (*beat*) Boys' room?

**GI**  Moving the car.

**MAIR**  Huh.

**GI**  Like what you've done with the curtains.

**MAIR**  It's the valance that makes it.

**GI**  Very handsome.

**MAIR**  It's the valance. (*beat*) That a new dress?

**GI**  First time on.

**MAIR**  Loehmann's?

**GI**  Oh, no! Wanamakers. There's a boutique shop. For young women. Upstairs. Know I shouldn't be spending the money 'cause things are tight 'cause Mickey's plant might be cutting back. But this boutique has the smartest things. Really pretty, bright colors. They have great stuff too for, you know, mature women. Call it their Silver Lady Closette, with an "e-t-t-e" at the end of the word "closet."

**MAIR**  Nothing wrong with a dress from Loehmann's. A good price and next to the Dine-O-Mat. Guess you're too busy steaming up vegetables to eat out?

**GI**  Don't really cook that much. 'Cause I been starting to paint a bit after work and all, just to be creative somehow and—

**MAIR**  Creating a home for a family, that's creative enough.

**GI**  Can't, uh, paint too much 'cause my job at the gift shop goes to six—

**MAIR**  Not drinking the root beer.

**GI**  It's a little flat. (*beat*) The others'll probably come by after the late mass.

**MAIR**  Guess you got to a real early one?

**GI**  My stomach was acting up. 'Sides, Mick usually goes for the both of us. (*beat*) He's been putting shelves up in the— "rec room" we're calling it. So if there's ever kids around they can wreck it up total and all.

**MAIR**  Probably why you couldn't make mass, on accounta wearing a dress that bright and all.

**GI**  Uh—

42

**MAIR**  Lord's day. Why there's an apostrophe-s at the end of the word "Lord's." Means it belongs to him.

**GI** (*beat*)  Mickey plans on getting by often as we can.

**MAIR**  Do what you can.

**GI**  Should be easy a while.

**MAIR**  It's a long drive to Lancaster Avenue.

**GI**  Should be easy, next few months.

**MAIR**  Not the same as it was when we moved in.

**GI**  Sure, but, just we expect things'll get a little hectic and—

**MAIR**  Used to be able to walk down the street at three A.M., you had to.

**GI**  Uh-huh—after a few months—

**MAIR**  Now there's a different type moving in. So I'd understand if you couldn't visit.

**GI**  No, no, it's just—

**MAIR**  Can't blame people, they don't wanna come.

**GI**  We plan on coming.

**MAIR**  Outta my hands, you don't wanna—

**GI**  Plan on visiting as often—

**MAIR**  You lead your own—

**GI**  I'm pregnant!

**MAIR** (*beat*)  Were the first family to have our own Frigidaire on Lancaster Avenue.

**GI** (*beat*)  I'm pregnant. Only three months along so—

**MAIR**   Only been married for two.

*A horn honks outside.*

**GI** (*beat*)   They're coming from GE today with our new fridge. Has its own defroster and everything.

**MAIR**   Won't waste time with a fridge like that. And seems to me you're the kind of person who don't waste too much time.

*Gi leaves Mair's parlor as Mickey enters his and Gi's living room. He has a can of beer in one hand, a Polaroid camera and balloons in the other. Gi enters, craddling an infant. It is six months later.*

**MICKEY**   Okay, okay, we're knocking a few around here. Leaning towards—

**GI**   "Stefan."

**MICKEY**   Right. After your father—but we don't like "Stefano."

**GI**   No.

**MICKEY**   So, Stefan after your father.

**GI**   Yes.

**MICKEY**   But—your dad's not dead.

**GI**   No, he's in Italy.

**MICKEY**   But see my dad's dead—so what'll I tell Mair?

**GI**   Just tell her we like the name "Carey" but . . .

**MICKEY**   We like the name "Carey" but . . . live babies don't always gotta be named after dead Irish people.

**GI**   For baptism we'll add the "Carey."

*The phone rings.*

**MICKEY** And for confirmation we'll use "Mickey."

**GI** "Michael."

**MICKEY** Ah—"Michael." (*going to phone*) I got it, I got it. (*answers phone*) Hey-ho! Hello, Mair. Nah, she never looked better. Yes, yeah s'true, Italians do have special enzymes in their skin. Yeah, born right on Gi's birthday, odds on that are—phew, forget it! So yeah, Gi, how old are you now?

**GI** Tell her I'm sleeping.

**MICKEY** She's twenty-four. (*to Gi*) Mair says she was fourteen when she had her first. Different world, Mair, yes it is. Look, look, we'll be 'round soon as things settle. There's a plant out Scranton looking for men.

**GI** I'm upstairs, asleep.

*Mickey puts the phone at Gi's ear.*

**GI** (*on phone*) Hello, Mair.

**MICKEY** Forgot your birthday!

**GI** (*on phone*) Fine, very easy.

**MICKEY** Was gonna fly you to France.

**GI** (*to Mickey*) Oh, well. (*on phone*) No, actually much easier than you told me.

**MICKEY** How 'bout a birthday picture?

**GI** (*on phone*) Uh-huh. Oh. In labor with Mickey eighteen hours, really? Ooh. I'm sorry to hear that. Ooh. That's awful. (*to Mickey*) You were born on the kitchen floor?

**MICKEY** Yeah, she was cooking dinner at the time.

*Mickey takes a photo.*

**GI** (*on phone*)  Well that's why I put the receipt in so you can just return it—"the Silver Closette." Next time I'll remember no bright colors. Yes, you're always in a lot of our thoughts too.

*She hangs up and Mickey snaps another photo.*

**GI**  C'mon, Mick.

**MICKEY**  C'mon with you!

**GI**  Kid's gonna think he's a celebrity a some kind. Kid's gonna think we're all famous, all these flashbulbs. We're not famous, nobody knows us but us.

**MICKEY**  And some other people.

**GI**  Some other people too but mostly only us know us.

**MICKEY**  Well, that's okay to know only a few people when you like them and life's going okay!

*Gi opens her shirt and offers her breast to the baby.*

**MICKEY** (*cont.*)  Oh.

**GI**  What, Mick?

**MICKEY**  That's not something—

**GI**  What?

**MICKEY**  Something you should be doing out in the open, right? Mean, 'cause I don't think I should be, while you're doing what you're doing there, I shouldn't be—

**GI**  Shouldn't be—?

**MICKEY**  Watching, you know.

**GI**   Don't mind.

**MICKEY**   Watching your breasts.

**GI**   Mickey?

**MICKEY**   Those are your breasts is all I'm saying.

**GI**   Well, sure.

**MICKEY**   Those are your breasts and they're bigger.

**GI**   'Cause a the milk.

**MICKEY**   Milk, sure, makes 'em bigger than they're usually.
Usually a nice size and all, not saying, but it's—

**GI**   Just a natural thing.

**MICKEY**   But's like—

**GI**   What?

**MICKEY**   S'like someone else is having all the fun.

**GI**   He's a baby!

**MICKEY**   Know he's a baby, just something about—

*She turns away from him.*

**MICKEY** (*cont.*)   C'mon, don't. (*He goes behind her and starts to
kiss her other breast.*)

**GI**   Don't do that, Mick.

**MICKEY**   What?

**GI**   It's confusing.

**MICKEY**   What?

**GI**   Don't, Mickey, c'mon, get out of there.

**MICKEY**   You could use a bottle instead.

**GI**  It's a natural thing, we decided!

**MICKEY**  *You* decided—

**GI**  I said, and you said, yeah.

*Mickey leaves the room.*

**GI** (*cont.*)  It's a natural thing and we decided and sometimes I'll have to be doing it in front of you is all. All it is. Just gotta get used to it—

*Mickey returns with his jacket.*

**GI** (*cont.*)  Where you off to?

**MICKEY**  Up the Grill.

**GI**  C'mon, no.

**MICKEY**  Wanna tell them!

**GI**  Not tonight, though.

**MICKEY**  Tell the boys!

**GI**  But come right back.

**MICKEY**  Just an hour. Up the Grill, see the boys, yut-ta-da.

**GI**  Okay, but come right back 'cause we're celebrating, right?

**MICKEY**  We're celebrating!

*He kisses her and goes. She calls after him.*

**GI**  Okay, but let them buy, 'cause it's your night! Bought all those drinks for Pip Mazzelli the night his wife had their eighth, that time. That woman's uterus's gonna put us in the poorhouse. You let Pip buy you some! Your night, Mick. Pip can afford it.

**MICKEY** (*off*)  We're celebrating!

**GI**   (*Gi looks around, alone now with her child.*) Gonna be beautiful. Gonna be strong and things will happen to you. You know, special things like events or something. 'Cause things will happen 'cause you're better than most. Putting a spell on you to be better than most. Poof. That's a spell word, magicians go "poof." And the spell is so's your . . . nose will be much nicer than mine. And so's . . . you'll have Mick's legs. That's the green-eyed man who was just here, giving me grief. He puts big steel beams together. And he's your father. Gotta know that at some point. And, uh, the more spell is you won't ever have acne ever . . . and'll have beautiful black hair without any silver in it till you're a famous old man who has to give lectures in Paris, France, and then looks good with silver hair so it'll be something you'll want to have. At these lectures you're giving you'll be communicating with all different types of people 'cause the world will be better by then. And they'll all be in the audience asking you about your mother and you'll go, yes, she was a great woman and famous artist but I am much more famous than her 'cause there's a spell on me. And besides, the best and only thing about her is she always had the most beautiful black hair that was nothing like the silver hair I now have on my head as I stand here at this podium. (*she cries*) Just crying all the time now and for no reason and it's the worse thing when you've got really nothing to cry about to be bawling like a baby. 'Cause if you start the baby bawling then everything gets really, really . . . soggy. (*beat*) We were the first on this block, except for the squirrels. We are . . . pioneers. (*beat*) Mick planted another rhododendron which means it's you, so you'll see it when you're older. You'll see so many things your whole life, 'cause I put a spell on you, Stefan Carey Michael. (*she kisses the baby*) No, don't drink my tears, you're not supposed to drink tears.

*Gi exits. Mickey comes on and enters "The Grill." He sits at a table with* JESSE. *He is thirty and African-American. It is five years later.*

**MICKEY** (*calling off*)   Who do we hafta kiss to get a drink around here?

**JESSE**   C'mon, Mick, you're gonna drown me!

**MICKEY**   Biggs, top us off! We're celebrating—Jesse's all the way from New Orleans. Boy, it's good to see a new face 'round here.

**JESSE**   But you haven't even touched the beignets I made.

**MICKEY**   Ben what?

**JESSE**   "Beignets." It's French for donut.

**MICKEY**   Yeah well, if I can't pronounce it, it don't belong in my mouth!

**JESSE**   Just a pastry, not gonna kill ya.

**MICKEY** (*he tastes*)   Not bad. Not bad at all. Guess I shouldn't be washing 'em down with beer though.

**JESSE**   Why not, everyone in New Orleans does it. And I must admit I was kinda famous for mine. So always dreamed of someday having my own business. Get this—Jesse's Joy Food!

**MICKEY**   Your own business, sure.

**JESSE**   Come up north, set it up. Stuff an entire neighborhood full of calories, fat, and sugar.

**MICKEY**   Now there's an idea—and you could make a killing offa Kelly, 'cause a the famous Kelly belly!

**JESSE**   Couldn't even think about it down south.

**MICKEY**   So here you are!

**JESSE**   Get ready to fall off your diet, Jesse's on the block!

**MICKEY**   Hoho!

*They toast and drink.*

**JESSE**   So, just the one kid?

**MICKEY**   That's all for now.

**JESSE**   Take him out for Halloween?

**MICKEY**   Oh sure, he's five, he eats that up.

**JESSE**   What he dress like?

**MICKEY**   Oh, some kinda, some kinda historical figure.

**JESSE**   (*beat*) George Washington?

**MICKEY**   Nah.

**JESSE**   Lincoln, bet—with the beard? Kids like Lincoln.

**MICKEY**   Nah, nuh.

**JESSE**   Jefferson, Franklin? Bet was Franklin—

**MICKEY**   Nuh-uh.

**JESSE**   FDR? Gave him a long cigarette?

**MICKEY**   Nah, was a black historical figure. (*pointing at Jesse's empty glass*) Top you off?

**JESSE**   Nuh, thanks.

**MICKEY**   S'on me?

**JESSE**  Thanks, fine. Black, huh?

**MICKEY**  You been sitting here with just an empty glass.

**JESSE**  Frederick Douglass?

**MICKEY**  (*calling off*)  Biggs, top us off!

**JESSE**  George Washington Carver.

**MICKEY**  Biggs?

**JESSE**  Joe Louis! The Brown Bomber?

**MICKEY**  (*beat*)  Harriet Tubman.

**JESSE**  C'mon.

**MICKEY**  Nuh.

**JESSE**  Your kid was—

**MICKEY**  Think that's weird?

**JESSE**  Well, s'not—

**MICKEY**  Nuh, c'mon? Think it's—?

**JESSE**  S'just not the usual Halloween costume.

**MICKEY**  (*beat*)  See his mother's always telling him stories outside a school and I'm telling her it's why we pay the extra money so the nuns can teach him right, you follow?

**JESSE**  Don't follow nothing where nuns are concerned. Those ladies scare the hell outta me—and I been to Mardi Gras.

**MICKEY**  Well we coulda sent him to the public school where all his friends go, but she wants him in the little suit and I think it's important to hear about Jesus and the rest of that crap. Let him decide later on if he buys any a it.

**JESSE**  Right?

**MICKEY**  And the wife's always off behind the nuns' back—
'cause that's what it is, behind their back—she's off telling
our kid other historical facts. And he gets a load of this
Underground Railroad business and kid thinks it's like his
model trains. So he paints all his little railroad—those
figurines that go in the little houses? He paints all them
black—

**JESSE**  Oh Jesus.

**MICKEY**  Okay, then puts them on the train and rides it
around the rec room. And then the wife gets on the Harriet
Tubman business and how she had a station on the
Underground Railroad and the kid goes ape 'cause he wants
to have a station on the Underground Railroad too.

**JESSE**  (*beat*)  Lemme get this straight—

**MICKEY**  All kindsa things to be on Halloween. Can be a,
you know, a ghost or something, can be a monster from
the deep, Spiderman—they got those flame-retardant—
my kid wants to be Harriet Tubman! So the wife made
a little turban. Locked himself in his room till I let
him dress up like Harriet Tubman. What can you
say?

**JESSE**  (*beat*)  Maybe next year he'll go as Lincoln.

**MICKEY**  Ah, but he's great—a little weird, takes after my
wife's family. But I gotta keep a roof over his head, weird
or not. So it's lucky I'm on my third interview for this nice
little position, not too shabby. It's not the welding but with
all the plants closing I fully intend to broaden my, you
know, whatnots.

**JESSE**   That's the thing, a man's gotta set himself up.

**MICKEY**   Keep abreast of the times.

**JESSE**   That's why, see, in the meantime I got this job at Penncorp Industries.

**MICKEY**   Penncorp?

**JESSE**   Found out today, they'll have me touring these airports, making reports.

**MICKEY**   Penncorp.

**JESSE**   Sorta surprised when they called so fast, but they said they been looking for a while in this area. But the man in the office said I'd be appropriate for the position, 'specially with the night school courses I signed up for.

**MICKEY**   Night school?

**JESSE**   They're gonna pay for them too. And as another kinda perk they give—can even get my flight license. Guess they haven't seen my driving record.

**MICKEY**   (*beat*)   Penncorp.

**JESSE**   Know that name?

**MICKEY**   Who don't? Company's buying up the whole town. Bringing in people from—you know, they're looking for a different type a guy. You getta bunch of the same guys together and, uh, the um, the work, the uh, output, they don't—don't always . . . You know, you'd think with all these young guys overseas there's gotta be tons a jobs. So I'm in no hurry. 'Cause every day I get closer to something new.

*A car horn honks outside. Gi enters. The horn honks again.*

**GI** (*calling outside*)   Stef, don't honk the horn.

**MICKEY**   Someone buy my old lady a drink!

**GI**   Why do boys love making loud sounds?

**MICKEY**   Someone buy my kid a drink!

**JESSE**   Gi?

**GI**   Jesse?

**MICKEY**   Someone buy ME a drink.

**JESSE**   Small world.

**MICKEY**   You two—?

**JESSE**   Met Gi at the market.

**GI**   What're you doing here, Jesse?

**JESSE**   Gettin' to know your husband, 'parently.

**GI**   Well, I thought my husband would be home earlier.

**MICKEY**   Ah, Gi, Jesse and me got to talking—

**GI**   Talking, that's what I figured. But you were supposed to watch the lunar orbit with Stefan?

**MICKEY**   Damn, right.

**GI**   And he asked me if you were in the rocket 'cause apparently you said that's where you'd be if anyone needed you. So I couldn't get Stef to go to sleep until I proved to him—(*horn honks, she calls out*)—your father is right here—until I proved you weren't becoming an astronaut.

**MICKEY**   And how do you know I'm not, young lady? We could be undergoing secret astronaut training right now.

**GI**   But about the job, Mick—

**MICKEY**   Not now, sweetheart.

**GI**   Just, the man at Penncorp called—

**MICKEY**   Okay, alright!

**GI** (*beat*)   It's just late, Mick.

**MICKEY**   I know, sweetheart, I know.

**GI**   Well—good seeing you, Jesse.

**JESSE**   You too, Gi.

**GI**   Be waiting in the car. (*Gi leaves.*)

**MICKEY**   You, uh, you got family?

**JESSE**   Been just me since I was little.

**MICKEY**   We . . . oughta have you over the house.

**JESSE**   Be gracious.

**MICKEY**   Gi cooks real good and you live nearby and we could have you over.

**JESSE**   Maybe should wait till things get better.

**MICKEY**   Whattaya mean?

**JESSE**   Just—things are tight for you, just said.

**MICKEY**   Things aren't tight. We got, you know, Gi works at the card shop and we get by—you come to dinner.

**JESSE**   Love to, Mick.

**MICKEY**   Gi's Italian and she makes a big meal. You know, peppers and onions, sausage, cheese, whatnot—we keep a jar of Alka-Seltzer by the door.

**JESSE**   Free this weekend.

**MICKEY**   Oh, you know. (*beat*) No, sure, but gotta ask Gi and all. She's got plans. Don't know her schedule. She makes things. Little things she paints.

**JESSE**   Whenever, Mick.

**MICKEY**   Just gotta ask Gi.

*Mickey leaves The Grill and arrives home to find Gi finishing a small painting on an easel in the kitchen. At first she does not acknowledge his presence. He takes his shirt off and wipes his face with it. It is midnight, five years later.*

**GI**   Sally Mazzelli said I should be glad you aren't young enough to be overseas fighting, least I got some idea you're somewhere in the neighborhood.

**MICKEY**   How was the party?

**GI**   He turned ten.

**MICKEY**   Was here for part of it.

**GI**   Five minutes is part of it.

**MICKEY**   Well, they were five jam-packed minutes, young lady. (*beat*) The kid was on me to make funny voices.

**GI**   It's very easy to make funny voices.

**MICKEY**   "Mommy's funny voices are good but yours stink."

**GI**   There's a pretty good funny voice right there.

**MICKEY**   Dont'cha wanna get some air?

**GI**   And if my funny voices are better it's because I practice them so I can talk to him.

**MICKEY** I'm here now, c'mon, young lady. Full moon out, whole thing—

**GI** His present?

**MICKEY** Got the kid a present, will you come on?

**GI** Not what he wanted.

**MICKEY** Every kid wants a baseball.

**GI** Not our kid.

**MICKEY** Every little boy—

**GI** Our little boy wanted a Talkie Tina.

**MICKEY** (*beat*) That's weird.

**GI** Be that as it may—

**MICKEY** So I'm supposed to get him that—?

**GI** You're supposed to be here for more than five minutes—

**MICKEY** A doll that wets her pants?

**GI** —during a huge picnic party—

**MICKEY** For a nine-year-old boy, a doll—?

**GI** TEN years old.

**MICKEY** Thank you very much, Miss Fountain of Information—

**GI** Stef's ten years old today.

**MICKEY** —I realize how old my kid is.

**GI** So it's not like he has to be in training for the World Series. And she talks, she doesn't wet her pants, she's Talkie Tina. Costs just as much as a baseball. Just . . . put some

58

clothes on, please. (*beat*) Couldn't even turn on the oven like I told you. Making the Hopalong Cake right now, midnight. He'll have it for breakfast.

**MICKEY** How 'bout I put the chairs out on the porch so we can—

**GI** I don't know where all those women can find the time to march all the way to Washington, D.C. I can barely find the energy to march from the bedroom to the kitchen twice a day.

**MICKEY** S'a lot of marching.

**GI** And if I'm really feeling energetic I march to the bathroom sometime in between.

**MICKEY** (*marching*) Didn't do that much marching myself in the high school band.

**GI** Don't stamp, you'll ruin the Hopalong Cake.

**MICKEY** (*stops marching*) Sound like my mother.

**GI** That's funny, don't think I can growl as well as she can. And I should know 'cause she spent the whole afternoon growling at little Ronnie Mazzelli.

**MICKEY** Ah, you know, she gets ornery.

**GI** Finally hid himself in the shrubs. I had to fish him out, cut myself all up.

**MICKEY** She ain't taking her heart medicine.

**GI** She just sat there, growling. All the other mothers brought her iced tea.

**MICKEY** Let's get some air—

**GI** She kept on insisting Jesse was the waiter.

**MICKEY** Seen the moon tonight? Let's sit on the porch.

**GI** It's too hot, all those bugs. (*beat*) Jesse said he's gonna bring by some citronella candles.

**MICKEY** (*beat*) Well, that's someone thinking.

**GI** Yes, and he promised Stef to take him flying once he gets his flight license. Which is nice, too, I think.

**MICKEY** Yeah, that's very, very nice.

**GI** (*beat*) I put the pillow in the rec room already. So you don't have to go up the stairs.

**MICKEY** (*beat*) You can smile at him but not in front of everybody. Still my house. Think you're being nice and modern or something and you just look funny all smiley like that with him.

**GI** (*beat*) Sometimes you fall up the stairs and I have to come out and get you and I'm tired tonight. So that's why I put the pillow directly in the rec room.

**MICKEY** This is my house.

**GI** You stand there saying that.

**MICKEY** Yes I do.

**GI** Can't believe you stand there saying that.

**MICKEY** This is my house.

**GI** I spend all afternoon lying to people—

**MICKEY** That's your business.

**GI** You're out picking up birthday candles—

**MICKEY**   You do what you do.

**GI**   After they just saw you all boozed up, could barely stand up in the grass and they all can smell it, the parents can smell it.

**MICKEY**   In your mind.

**GI**   Me telling them lies, them knowing I'm lying, looks on their faces.

**MICKEY**   Only look was on your face, that look to me like something I did. And what did I do?

**GI**   Nothing.

**MICKEY**   What did I do just standing there?

**GI**   Nothing, you did nothing.

**MICKEY**   That's right.

**GI**   All the time standing there like a idiot and me running around—

**MICKEY**   'Cause I don't know!

**GI**   You don't know is right. Sleep on the couch unless it's one of those nights you're friendly and even then come in bed and nothing! Nothing.

**MICKEY**   I can do something. (*he smears her painting*) That's what I can do. I did that. There you go, I did something, right?

*A moment passes in silence.*

**GI**   Just wanted a nice party.

**MICKEY** (*beat*)   But shouldn'ta spent all this money—just a birthday. China plates, what have you. My family didn't have nothing either and we were fine, my brothers, sisters. What kids can do for a family—they can help out. In the kitchen, all around. Stef should have a brother.

**GI**  We're out of money.

**MICKEY**  Or a sister.

**GI**  You drink.

**MICKEY**  Just got all this time on my hands!

**GI**  (*beat*)  Card shop all day, here all night—I don't have time for friends.

**MICKEY**  Lookit, I'll help, do something. Hit the pavement, take the night school, whatever. And if things go really ace then maybe, could maybe think about another one. Little brother for Stef? You're still young.

**GI**  I am?

**MICKEY**  And I feel like a kid.

**GI**  (*beat*)  Someday I want a nice party. All of us there, all being nice. Everyone around, place looking nice. Peaceful. (*beat*) Where'd you go? All those hours—

**MICKEY**  Come outside.

*He leaves. She calls out to him.*

**GI**  Called every place I knew! It's my birthday too. Don't suppose you remembered—it's my—

*Music swells from outside. Gi goes to the window and colored lights wash over her face. Mickey reenters with a box of candy.*

**MICKEY**  Those are Christmas lights.

**GI**  In the trees!

**MICKEY**   I shaped 'em like the Eiffel Tower. Spent all afternoon at Kelly's puttin' it together. It's your birthday too.

**GI**   Mick. Mickey . . . I don't know.

*He goes to kiss her and after a moment she accepts as they kiss. Mair comes on and sits with her bag at a table set for Thanksgiving. Jesse enters and stands next to her, holding a wrapped plate of pastries. Mickey and Gi stop kissing when they realize they're no longer alone. Mickey goes off. Gi moves into the dining room, arranging food on the table. Music starts to blare from a room on the second floor. It is three years later.*

**GI** (*calling upstairs*)   Stefan, come down! We're going to have a very peaceful dinner.

**JESSE**   That's alright, Gi.

**GI**   Jesse's here. He brought been—

**JESSE**   Beignets.

**GI**   They're French.

**JESSE**   And cannolis for Gi.

**GI**   Haven't seen him in a while!

**MAIR**   I'm here too.

**GI**   Your Mair's here too!

**MAIR**   Boy says I stare at him.

**GI**   That's just the way your Mair is, Stefan. You can stare back at her if it makes you feel better!

*A door slams upstairs, muffling the music.*

**JESSE** He'll come down. You know his tricks.

**MAIR** What's in his ear?

**GI** Don't know, Mair, why don't you ask him?

**JESSE** She means his earring.

**GI** His earring, Mair, he got it last year at the Bicentennial (*calling upstairs*)—you can tell her.

**MAIR** Got a commemorative plate from the Bicentennial, you want that, Gi?

**GI** I don't need any more commemorative plates—

**MAIR** How old's that kid anyway?

**JESSE** Stef's thirteen now?

**GI** You know that, Mair. Just had his grade school graduation, Mair, you were at it. We picked you up for it. That day that was so busy and we had to pick you up because you won't take the bus since you weren't taking your medication and had that attack and smashed up your car? So we picked you up and you came over and ate all that cake. All that cake we had set aside for the friends that you ate before they got here?

**MAIR** I could move into that room you got me in.

**GI** That's the rec room.

**MAIR** So you wouldn't have to shuttle me around all the time.

**GI** Oh, but we like keeping you on the run.

**MAIR** (*to Jesse*) Your family people ever put their old folks on the street?

**JESSE** Nah, we'd just float 'em up the river.

64

**GI**  You're not out on the street. Not yet you aren't.

**MAIR**  Why didn't you have more kids, Gi?

**JESSE**  (*beat, then to Gi*)  You need any help?

**GI**  No, thank you, I'll take that, Jesse. You sit.

**JESSE**  You smoking, Gi?

**GI**  Just real quick puffs, to get my bearings. Mair, please take your old bag off my nice table.

*Gi exits with Jesse's pastries.*

**MAIR**  (*beat*)  You make baked goods?

**JESSE**  Just recently got a little storefront—Jesse's Joy Food.

**GI**  (*off*)  He makes cakes, Mair!

**MAIR**  Pipe down!

**JESSE**  Should drop in.

**MAIR**  Not big on desserts myself. Don't you got family?

**GI**  (*off*)  Jesse's an orphan, Mair.

**MAIR**  Pretty old to be an orphan. Married?

**JESSE**  Busy with the shop. But I'm always looking for that special lady.

*After a moment, Gi reenters.*

**GI**  Jesse's been our neighbor for eight years now, you know that. He's got his own bakery and he makes all kinda cakes he learned how to make in New Orleans.

**MAIR**  We been discussing it.

**JESSE**  But I used to fly in a 'copter.

**GI** And his job used to have him in a helicopter.

**MAIR** Don't have to talk to me like I'm five.

**GI** (*beat*) You meet every year at Stefan's birthday when you always think Jesse's a waiter.

**MAIR** Is Stef's earring supposed to mean something or something?

**JESSE** Kids today—

**GI** Just means Stef likes an earring in his ear.

**JESSE** They all got 'em.

**GI** They all do, right, Stef? (*calling upstairs*) Just why don't we answer her, she gets unpleasant and I get upset and people get loud and why don't you just tell your Mair you just like it is all. Stefan? That's all there is to it.

**MAIR** I'm in the house, you know.

**GI** Yes, for a week you're in the house on your holiday. And you'll be at Molly's a week at Christmas, which is very nice.

**MAIR** He like that thing in his ear?

**GI** Is it hot in here or is it me?

**MAIR** I'm freezing.

**JESSE** Sit a moment, Gi.

**GI** It's just I'm cooking and I'm just a little warm with the, uh—

**JESSE** Sure.

**GI** It's just hard coordinating all this meal. It's got all these elements.

66

**JESSE**  Sit a minute.

**GI** (*she does*)  And it's warm in the house now.

**JESSE**  I'll open the back door. (*Jesse goes.*)

**GI**  And I was late starting today 'cause the squirrels in the attic keep me up at night, they must be telling all their friends. They climb up the rhododendron 'cause Mickey keeps forgetting to clip the shrubs, they reach right up to the gutter. Then was at the desk all morning with the charcoals Stefan got me, which I really think I'll be able to use—

*Jesse returns.*

**JESSE**  Should be some air now.

**MAIR**  Now I'm really freezing.

**GI**  I'd like to duplicate this painting I saw, the museum in town had a painting called *Nude Descending the Staircase*.

**MAIR**  Sweet Lord.

**GI**  It's a wonderful painting, all cut up in little bits, like.

**MAIR**  Made one just like it at the senior citizen center with construction paper and scissors.

**GI**  All the people were staring at it and for a moment you knew everyone there.

**JESSE**  Like they weren't strangers.

**GI**  Yeah.

**MAIR**  Oh brother. Did you make the centerpiece?

**GI**  I did! Just a Pilgrim and an Indian.

**MAIR**   That's a Pilgrim?

**GI**   Yes. Yes it is.

**JESSE**   Sure it is. How 'bout those Pilgrims? They decided to get along with the native tribes so they could all have a nice meal together, get to know each other, break bread—which is quite a story if you think about it.

**MAIR**   When do we get turkey?

**GI**   When Mickey gets back from the State Store, which should be just—soon. So we're waiting for Mick.

**MAIR**   Hell could freeze—

**GI**   (*calls upstairs*)   We're waiting for your father. (*Gi pours giblets onto Mair's plate.*)

**GI**   You can tide yourself over with biscuits, giblets—

**MAIR**   Ew.

**JESSE**   You don't like giblets?

**MAIR**   Bird guts, all it is.

**GI**   Just a gravy.

**MAIR**   Yeah, but who knows.

**GI**   Piping hot!

**MAIR**   They come in this little packet, plastic inside the turkey and who knows what's in it.

**GI**   We know what's in it.

**JESSE**   It's just they wrap the insides after they kill it.

**GI**   And Jesse'd know 'cause he's a cook—

**MAIR**   Carey used to kill the bird in our backyard, so we knew what was in it and whatever it was—

**GI**   Just giblets.

**MAIR**   —weren't plastic, tell you that much.

**GI**   Hell, they're just giblets!

*She slams down the ladle, splattering gravy on Mair.*

**MAIR**   You sprayed me, Gi!

**JESSE**   I got it. (*taking the ladle*)

**MAIR**   Sprayed me with giblets.

**GI**   You don't hafta eat it.

**MAIR**   Got giblets sprayed on my dress. Molly bought me this dress 'cause I got too many bright ones from Gi, and it's for Christmas too and lookit it.

**GI**   Christ.

**MAIR**   Sweet heaven!

**GI**   Sorry, it's just—(*to Jesse*) Mair don't—

**MAIR**   Mair don't appreciate the mouth she's been developing over the years. The words, the cursing—

*A car is heard pulling up outside.*

**JESSE**   There's Mickey now.

**MAIR**   It's not something you wanna hear flying around a house.

**GI**   Stef, your father's here!

**MAIR**   You say God's name like that before a sentence, he expects you're talking to him and he listens. When he finds out you aren't speaking to him he gets riled up!

69

**GI**   Wasn't speaking TO God.

**MAIR**   *I* get riled up! S'given you a roof over your family's head.

**GI**   Yes.

**MAIR**   A fine, sick-free body.

**GI**   Yes he has.

**MAIR**   And a husband what pays your bills.

**GI**   Mickey don't work, I do.

**MAIR**   (*beat*)   Had some trouble, not his fault. Always provided for you, best he knows. Had a choice, could provide for me or provide for you. He chose you.

**JESSE**   I should open another window, maybe.

**MAIR**   Great, I'll be a icicle.

**GI**   Mick said he'd help put the storm windows in 'fore winter but he hasn't gotten to it.

MICKEY *enters, very happy and very drunk.*

**MICKEY**   Heard my name!

**GI**   Just saying about the storm windows—

**MICKEY**   Jesse . . . ?

**JESSE**   Mickey, hi.

**GI**   Jesse's joining us, remember? Haven't seen him in forever practically and I called to order the pie and—

**JESSE**   And I invited myself.

**MICKEY**   Well, Jesse, you know, me casa es your casa.

**GI**   Mick, thought we all could have a very peaceful dinner.

**MAIR**   So when's the turkey?

**MICKEY**   If we can't have Turkey Day together—

**GI** (*calling*)   Stef!

**MICKEY**   Oh we just had the best time. We had the—look at you! Gi, this table.

**GI**   Okay. We're about to have a very peaceful—

**MICKEY**   This table looks fit for a Pilgrim. I am Captain Pocahanas and you are my Pilgrims!

**MAIR** (*pointing to the centerpiece*)   Gi says this is a Pilgrim.

**MICKEY**   That's a Pilgrim?

**GI**   Sit down, Mick, we'll get started.

**JESSE**   Sure, we'll get—

**MICKEY** (*going to kiss Gi*)   Give me a—

**GI**   Your breath, Mick.

**MICKEY**   Don't give me one then.

*Mair kisses him.*

**MICKEY**   Where's the boy?

**GI**   He's painting a mural. Up on his ceiling. Of Gertrude Stein.

**MAIR**   That some girlfriend?

**MICKEY**   That boy is the spitting image of—his mother. Don't you think, Jesse?

**JESSE** I'dunnuh know, Mickey, always thought he took after—

**MICKEY** (*to Gi*) Did that to get me, right? Gave him that face to get me, I know.

**MAIR** Stef's got a Jewish girlfriend?

**GI** No, Mair.

**MICKEY** Gave him your face when I wasn't looking, put a spell on him, something.

**MAIR** Pipe down and cut the turkey.

*Mickey salutes her and sits.*

**GI** Okay, here we are.

**JESSE** Yes we are.

**GI** Just dish it out, then we'll start.

**MAIR** You'll say grace and then we'll start!

**MICKEY** You can say grace, Mair, 'cause of the loveliness of the tone of your voice.

**MAIR** (*bows her head*) Bless us oh Lord and these thy gifts which we are about to receive from thy bounty through Christ, our Lord—(*to Gi*) I'm talking to HIM here—amen.

**MICKEY** Here's the meat, let's eat.

**MAIR** Never mind.

**JESSE** Looks great, Gi.

**MICKEY** It's a spread!

**JESSE** S'hard to make.

72

**GI**  Thank you, Jesse.

**MICKEY**  I think it looks great too!

**GI**  Mick, why don't you start carving.

**MAIR**  Tell me, Jesse, your people eat a lot of green beans?

**JESSE**  Uh—

**GI**  Mair, you start passing, 'kay?

**JESSE**  I like green beans.

**MAIR**  Got this theory, no one agrees—

**GI**  Mair, you start passing, please, okay?

**MICKEY**  (*trying to carve the turkey*)  Whole crowd was up at The Grill tonight. Biggs, Mazzelli—think they'd all be home with their families, what have you, but the whole gang was out. Kelly was there with his belly.

**JESSE**  Man, that guy's wide around. Gi, you should see his—

**MICKEY**  Well, he's fat.

**MAIR**  You got the beets from last year?

**GI**  Sure, Mair.

**MICKEY**  Hey! Kelly's belly is famous—until he had this operation and lost his belly but we still talk about Kelly's belly, and call him it too.

**GI**  Mickey, you gotta pass too.

**MICKEY**  And the looker on his arm tonight!

**MAIR**  Want some beets.

**GI**  Mick—

**MICKEY**  You got 'em, Mair o' mine. Redheaded lady, looker, all the heads turned, chink-chink-chink. My head stayed in its place, Gi, but all the heads turned, chink-chink.

*He gestures with the knife.*

**JESSE**  Careful.

**MICKEY**  I see it. And we're going on, shooting the—

*He gestures with the knife again.*

**GI**  Careful!

**MICKEY**  I see it, backseat driver. Hew-hew! So, yeah, anyway, we're talking, hoisting a few . . . elbows, speculating on how Kelly, with or without his belly, cause Kelly ain't a looker himself with or without it, right? We're speculating on how he nabbed this one with the . . . hair. The whole look. So Hughie Walsh—mouth on this guy— Walshie just screams it out, goes, loud as all—goes, "Hey, Kelly! Aren't you dating over your head on the food chain?" (*laughs loudly*) Oh, and Kelly goes beet red, purple, blue, turns every color in the coloring book 'cause it turns out—this chick's his sister. And her name's Shelly!

**MAIR**  Shelly Kelly.

**MICKEY**  The name's Shelly Kelly!

**MAIR**  Just said it!

**MICKEY**  It's his goddam sister!

**GI**  Mick, Mair don't like the language—

**MAIR**  Dark meat, please.

**MICKEY**  Oh, we had a laugh outta that, let me tell ya—

**GI**   Where's Stefan?

**MICKEY**   And she is so—and Kelly's pretty ugly, pretty hard to face except without a few in you, which we had, did I mention it?

**GI**   Once or twice, Mick.

**MICKEY**   And we were all talking, she's a nice gal, Shelly. She's interested what everyone's doing, okay, me and her get to shooting the—

**MAIR**   Dark meat!

**MICKEY**   —get to talking. She's going on, alls she ever wanted, meet the right guy and all, okay? But they're all just interested in her . . . they like her hair. How she dresses, whatnot. So—buy her a drink, Mickey, I'm thinking. Well, ladies drink free on Thursday but I pretend to buy her one, okay. 'Cause she seems like she needs someone to pretend just a bit, so I do it. We talk some more, yu-ta-da. Haven't talked to anyone new—all the same old faces. So it's good to talk to a new person every once in a—told her about Gi, the boy. Pictures in my wallet. And Kelly's asleep in his beer for, you know, an hour at this point, so I volunteer to take her home.

**MAIR**   No one's passing the beets.

**MICKEY**   Walk her to her door.

**JESSE**   Mick.

**MICKEY** (*beat*)   So Shelly thought this was sweet. Nothing for me. But felt sweet. I felt sweet. Haven't felt sweet . . . in years. And I go in her place, real sweet for a single girl and there we are so I go . . . go . . . , "Who do I have to kiss to get a drink around here?"

**GI** (*looking upstairs*)   Won't come down.

**MICKEY**   And she smiled. (*beat*) Haven't seen a smile like that in . . . don't know how long. (*beat*) So I kissed her. (*beat*) But she didn't back. We seemed to be getting on and all but guess 'cause . . . 'cause I told her about Gi, the boy.

**GI**   Stefan.

**MICKEY**   KNOW his name. And how I can't keep a job for my family to have anything, 'cause there aren't any jobs to keep. And how Gi likes nice stuff. How I drink away the little we got, how we owe everyone, and no one wants a welder, cause a machines—and I was a big, capable welder—and, and how we just had the one kid 'cause a . . . some reason or other. You know, I love kids. Feel like one myself, told her. And kissed her little. Told her everything while I kissed her little. (*beat*) Gonna go to bed now. And in the morning guess I'll be moving away. Like I mentioned'd probably be best thing for everyone involved. Did I mention that? Probably once or twice, Mick.

*Mickey goes out. His footsteps are heard on the stairs.*

**GI**   The lights're off on the stairs 'cause we're supposed to be conserving energy.

*Silence except for the sound of Mair eating.*

**MAIR**   What?

**GI**   Shit.

**MAIR**   Mother of Mercy!

**GI**   Please.

**JESSE**   It's only a word, Mrs.—

**GI**   Just—don't.

**MAIR**   You believe this mouth?

**GI**   Just a word for Chrissake!

**MAIR**   Jesus, Mary and—!

**GI**   Just a word until someone judges your entire character by it.

**MAIR**   Oh, brother.

**GI**   Suggesting you're something you're not.

**JESSE**   Gi?

**GI**   Or something you thought you'd never end up being!

**MAIR**   Just pass the beets!

*Gi throws the tureen of beets on the floor. A moment passes.*

**GI**   You don't hafta eat beets at Thanksgiving anyway. There's other vegetables. Please eat the vegetables. Spent my whole day doing nothing but making vegetables.

**JESSE**   I'll eat the vegetables, Gi.

**GI**   You will?

**MAIR**   I'll eat 'em too.

**GI**   'Preciate it.

**MAIR**   I'll make sure and leave most of the green beans for Jesse, though.

*End of Act One.*

# ACT TWO

*It is three years later. Just after midnight. Gi stands next to the bathroom door, holding a man's bathrobe.*

**GI**  Towel's on the rack. Pink one, says Holiday Inn? Weird having you in the house. Not weird, 'course, you've been in the house before. Just after such a long time. Stefan won't—probably won't be here tonight, so you can stay in his room. He's spending a lot of time at this summer theater. They're doing *Bye Bye Birdie* but setting it in Germany in the thirties, for some reason I don't get. He's explained it to me. He's getting school credit for it, which I really don't get. And he has all these new friends, I can't keep up. They're very creative. So, yeah, so you can sleep there, on accounta how weird the situation is. There's an extra toothbrush I put out, the blue one. The comedy and tragedy masks on it? Got it for Stef but he never used it for some reason he won't tell me. He's got all these secrets all of a sudden. *(beat)* Stefan stays at this one friend's house, this boy? This boy's all hairy and big, he's matured faster than the rest, but he always says "thank you" when he's over. That's a sign of something when you're sixteen. They have sleepovers. So I'm here a lot and he's not. *(beat)* That awful scene. *(laughs a little)* Thanksgiving is a holiday and we had that awful scene. Still a stain after three years! *(beat)* You brought beignets. And with what happened tonight and still you thought to bring beignets.

*Jesse comes out of the bathroom with his hand bandaged.*

**JESSE**  Just showed up on your doorstep.

**GI**  *(taking his hand)*  Let me see.

**JESSE**  Didn't even call—

**GI**   Anyone'd do the same.

**JESSE**   Don't know about that.

**GI**   Any friend would, sure.

**JESSE**   And it's late—

**GI**   I'll make some . . . tea?

**JESSE** (*stops her*)   Known you ten years.

**GI**   Flies. (*beat*) You know, all the different type a families moving in—it's a whole different neighborhood. Different, you know, cultures, and it's bound to be, at times, it's bound to be—

**JESSE**   Yeah, nuh.

**GI**   They were just kids.

**JESSE**   Nuh, sure.

**GI**   Teenagers.

**JESSE**   Uh-huh.

**GI**   All they are. Having fun, they get out of hand, one bad apple—

**JESSE**   Things were finally going good with the shop.

**GI**   But you're insured.

**JESSE**   Will cost some on top of the reimbursement. Said they'd send someone 'round tomorrow. Measure the pane. Then ship the glass, day after next.

**GI**   So there.

**JESSE** (*beat*)   Brought my own toothbrush so I didn't end up using the one with the faces.

**GI**  Should just throw the thing out.

**JESSE**  Just for tonight, Gi.

**GI**  Long as you need.

**JESSE**  All my cakes had glass in them.

**GI** (*beat*)  There's an extra pillow on the dresser. Right under the mosaic Stef made from all Mair's commemorative plates. One day things got a little unpleasant and I had to throw a few of them. Then Stef asked if he could keep the pieces. The mosaic's in the shape of a bull because Stef's a Taurus. Go in at night to see if Stef's home and forget it's there and the bull shape scares the hell outta me. That's silly. Think it's an animal in the dark. 'Cause a Mickey's always jumped out from behind the furniture. He'd do this growl. S'living in those little apartments behind Aronamink. An efficiency. They say it's an efficiency but it's so tiny I don't see how he can move around in it to make it efficient. Had me up. Says he's off it, but's always a six in the fridge. He's taking a typing course, which is funny to imagine Mickey behind one a those. Here's his robe he left. For the morning. (*beat*) You know, every day I get up and Stefan runs in and out to God knows where. Then I go out and wave to all the ladies on the street, but they have their girlfriends, and they think I'm too particular, or something—I heard one of them say it once. And since I've been promoted to manager at the gift shop, I'm stuck back in a tiny office and there's only the phone. And the staff says I drive them crazy when I'm out talking all the time, which I don't think I am talking all the time. But you come over, every now and then a visit, and guess what I'm saying is . . . you were always supportive of my stuff, my little paintings I make, and, um, I know it's bad circumstances but s'good to see you. (*beat*) I'll go put on the tea.

**JESSE** (*beat*)  Was a lady I knew.

**GI**  Uh-huh.

**JESSE**  Just before I moved up? She lived under where I stayed. Always baking things. All the smells'd float up. She was always bringing me sandwiches and things she'd bake 'cause she was worried I wasn't eating.

**GI**  Sweet a her.

**JESSE**  I was eating, but she knew when you're only the one you don't cook too much.

**GI**  Right? I've got all this Tupperware in the fridge. Little, half-eaten things. Piles up.

**JESSE**  I was living near the Quarter, so—people drinking, spilling out onto the street. Whenever things got too loud, she'd come up the back stairs, sit with me. Outside it was crazy, but inside we'd be making pastries. Beignets, cannolis and such. We'd close our eyes, try not to hear, just smell the pastry smells. Then pretend we were in some fancy shop in Paris, or Italy. When it all got quiet she'd go back downstairs, leaving me with all the things we'd made.

**GI**  She sounds sweet.

**JESSE**  One night after it got quiet, and she's gone back home, I went down to her place, stood at her door, hours it seemed, practicing speeches—"Knock, Jesse, just knock." Finally I . . . I went back upstairs. Without knocking, without saying a word.

**GI** (*beat*)  You'll meet another nice lady someday.

**JESSE**  Maybe.

**GI**  Could happen.

**JESSE**  Hard to come by.

**GI**  Far between.

**JESSE**  Don't meet them every day.

**GI**  You'd be overrun! And then there wouldn't be time to—bake.

**JESSE**  You're nice, Gi.

**GI**  No. I'm . . . middle-aged. (*beat*) Left your window open in there. Gets stuffy. Just a tiny room and once anyone's breathing in it for just a little bit of time, well—

**JESSE**  Should be fine.

**GI**  Stefan can sleep in the rec room if he comes in. Left him a note on the kitchen table.

**JESSE**  'Preciate it.

**GI**  Anyone woulda. Mickey woulda insisted. (*beat*) If you didn't put in the storm windows don't know what I woulda done. (*beat*) If you need anything just rap on the door. Don't rap loudly or I'll jump. I'm a light sleeper—cause a all the squirrels in the humane traps in the attic. I'm too scared to take them out and release them so I been feeding them. So now I guess they're pets. A couple just had babies, they're cute when they're little. But they keep me awake—and there's talk a putting in a train line through the back someday so then no one'll ever get a wink of sleep. But, so, if you rap—

**JESSE**  Gi?

**GI**  Things happen real quick and all, just like that. Then the whole business changes overnight. That'll be soon.

**JESSE**  Soon.

**GI**  Yes.

**JESSE**  Change.

**GI**  Sure.

**JESSE**  Gi.

**GI**  Uh-huh?

*They kiss.*

**GI**  (*beat*)  This isn't my real hair. You can't tell anyone. It's all silver underneath. Like an old lady's. Can you believe it? 'Cause mostly I feel about the farthest thing from an old lady as I can mostly get.

*They exit as Mickey and Mair enter a room in a nursing home. Mair stands holding her bag and a rosary, wearing her coat. Mickey sits on a chair holding a small cake. It is two years later.*

**MAIR**  I'm not singing so don't expect a song.

**MICKEY**  Fine, Mair, don't gotta—

**MAIR**  And only got two candles. Just don't expect a song.

**MICKEY**  Okay, no song.

**MAIR**  And it's coconut.

**MICKEY**  Just siddown.

**MAIR**  So, happy birthday.

**MICKEY**  Thanks.

**MAIR**  Two candles're enough anyway to light on such a small cake. Small cake on account a it's just us two here 'swhy it's small.

**MICKEY**  Must be a classy club if they only let us in.

**MAIR**  Yeah, well, I stole it from the cafeteria when I was supposed to be playing bingo. Some old lady turning a hundred, won't even know it's gone. (*looks out window*) Get by those protesters on the way in?

**MICKEY**  Just a handful.

**MAIR**  Scaring everyone away with their pictures of old people.

**MICKEY**  Don't pay 'em any mind.

**MAIR**  Old people hooked up to machines.

**MICKEY**  What's with the coat, Mair?

**MAIR**  And who knows where Molly is. She didn't appreciate some remark I made at your aunt Nan's viewing. Everyone expects me to roll over and die real sweet. But I got my bag packed and believe you me, I'm gonna use it. Want some root beer?

**MICKEY**  Nuh, Mair, sit down.

**MAIR**  You want it, you're just not saying it. (*remembering*) Don't got any.

**MICKEY**  Don't want any!

**MAIR**  Believe that fridge?

**MICKEY**  Will you siddown?

**MAIR**  Only fits a few plates.

**MICKEY**  Gi and me saw this guy balancing plates.

**MAIR**  Broke my commemorative plate of that movie star's inauguration.

**MICKEY**  At this circus we saw.

**MAIR**  Light your candles.

**MICKEY**  That Ringling Brothers.

**MAIR**  Hate the circus.

**MICKEY**  He had 'em on his feet and his face, his nose—

**MAIR**  All those mean animals.

**MICKEY**  —the end a poles he had strapped to his back or something. And they were all turning fast to the music like.

**MAIR**  That's not the way to treat animals, all cooped up. 'Cause you know, they do. They coop 'em up.

**MICKEY**  Were up close so Gi was trying to see if they were china plates or what, or just, you know, plates.

*He lights the sole candle on the cake.*

**MAIR**  You eat tonight?

**MICKEY**  Yeah, yeah—and I said why'd he use china plates? Case he drops one, what then?

**MAIR**  Make a wish, blow 'em out.

*He blows out the candle.*

**MICKEY**  And she was thinking it's more scary if they're nice plates. She's always going on about china plates, silverware, stuff like that. I don't see, myself, I don't see the difference. People can eat on anything, right?

**MAIR**  You're just drinking, that's no good.

**MICKEY**  Ate my dinner, will you c'mon!

**MAIR**  Nobody ever survived just drinking.

**MICKEY**  Not drinking two weeks now!

**MAIR**  You come here and sit with me and eat.

**MICKEY**  It's a rest home.

**MAIR**  What you and Molly pay for it, they can feed you too.

**MICKEY**  I eat fine.

**MAIR**  Seen the receipt. Molly showed me. T'make sure I'm grateful enough when she finally visits.

**MICKEY**  It's only Molly pays for it. The other place was nicer but I lost the job, why we couldn't—

**MAIR**  Not complaining.

**MICKEY**  Everyone's talking 'bout things getting better in the country—

**MAIR**  Am I complaining?

**MICKEY**  But I'm still outta work, so it's only Molly who's paying now.

**MAIR**  Pipe down. I'm a kind lady, you don't know it. Got soft insides too, like yourself. You don't hold the patent on soft insides.

**MICKEY**  Take your pills today?

**MAIR**  Was kind when I met your father, a kind young woman. Voice like a nightingale. Now I hear what they call me.

**MICKEY**  Will you take a load off?

**MAIR**  What Stefan's friends called me that time I was over.

**MICKEY**  In your mind.

**MAIR**  "Godzilla." Heard it. Heard from him?

86

**MICKEY**  He moved up the city after high school, nuh. Every now and then sends a letter to Gi, what he's doing. Then she calls and tells me what's in them. Don't know why he doesn't write me himself.

**MAIR**  Write a letter, get a letter. My motto.

**MICKEY**  But guess he's busy.

**MAIR**  'Cept if you're writing Molly, forget it.

**MICKEY**  What with his activities and all.

**MAIR**  Hell could freeze over 'fore you get a response. She wants to know why I don't call her up on the phone. Runs into money! Said they'd bill me a dollar a call here! Think Molly'll ever think to call me?

**MICKEY**  Molly's busy! (*beat*) Just want for Stefan what I had with Gi. And he's real popular with the girls from the pictures he sends me. Gi thinks they're just friends but I know my boy. He likes girls. Figured I'd be planting another rhododendron by now, but most kids today—he's young! He's just having a good time.

**MAIR**  We never had a good time and if we did we knew something was up.

**MICKEY**  Oh and get this—he's taking a course on how to be a Buddha, or something.

**MAIR**  Jesus Lord.

**MICKEY**  Ah, he's just—

**MAIR**  Can they teach you that?

**MICKEY**  Kid's always been—Gi always says he's gonna do what he wants—

**MAIR**  Gi's the expert.

**MICKEY**  Just like her. Says what she wants, does what she wants. Not gonna stop her! Her life. Who am I? (*beat*) Mean, I could fit there. That room off the back. Rec room. Made it myself. If she'd have me. Wouldn't have to sleep upstairs. If she'd have me.

**MAIR**  Heard she's going with him.

**MICKEY**  Ahh—

**MAIR**  Molly said she heard from a frienda hers, neighbor of Gi's—

**MICKEY**  You know.

**MAIR**  The neighbor says Gi's gone days on end and someone saw the two downtown together.

**MICKEY**  Yeah, she's going with him.

**MAIR**  Just gotta stand up for what's yours. Tried to build you up, encourage you. Things you couldn't even do I'd tell you you could do 'em. Look the spitting image of Carey. Sometimes when you visit, if I didn't know, if it was later at night and my head wasn't so clear, I'd suspect Carey'd come back. You ain't Carey though?

**MICKEY**  Mick.

**MAIR**  Always thought I'd go first . . .

**MICKEY**  It's Mickey.

**MAIR**  If I was having one of my bad days, like I been . . . Carey . . . all the time . . .

**MICKEY**  Mair, it's Mickey.

**MAIR** (*beat*)  Never even fixed that shelf in the kitchen on Lancaster Avenue.

**MICKEY**  Meant to.

**MAIR**  Always over to Gi's fixing things, and she's going with that man and jars fell off and I cut my hand.

**MICKEY**  Meant to fix it.

**MAIR**  CUT MY HAND.

**MICKEY**  You take your medicine?

**MAIR**  Don't wanna be hooked up to no machine.

**MICKEY** (*beat*)  C'mon, will you sit?

**MAIR**  Your father, that awful way.

**MICKEY**  You take your pills?

**MAIR**  Machines now can keep you forever. But made my peace with Jesus and I know you don't buy Jesus but don't matter 'cause he buys you.

**MICKEY**  Come on, Mair.

**MAIR**  No machines. Just say it, Mickey, so an old lady can go to bed.

**MICKEY**  Lotta nonsense.

**MAIR**  Just say it so I can stop asking.

**MICKEY**  Lotta . . . hooey.

**MAIR**  Just sleep. S'all I want. Good night's sleep. (*beat*) Don't like this room. No view.

**MICKEY**  Just keep with your medicine.

**MAIR**  You gotta grow up and do something, Mick.

**MICKEY**  (*beat*)  Maybe we can change your room, you don't like it. Should be more cash soon—I'm taking this data entry course now which would put me in line for—I'll talk to that lady in the office, some curtains, see what I can—

**MAIR**  Window needs a valance.

**MICKEY**  See if we can change the room. To a brighter one or—

**MAIR**  Mmhm.

**MICKEY**  'Course it might be . . . might be hard at this point.

*Mickey exits. Gi appears in a room in Stefan's city apartment. Music and sounds of a party are heard. Mickey reenters in a suit. He approaches Gi. It is five years later.*

**MICKEY**  Took the bus up?

**GI**  Splurged on the train. Still spending like I got it.

**MICKEY**  Sample the finger foods?

**GI**  Had some spanakopita.

**MICKEY**  Yeah, what's that?

**GI**  It's Greek for spinach pie.

**MICKEY**  Yeah, well, it's all Greek to me. Didn't try any of it 'cause I didn't recognize any of it. Want some punch? Not much kick to it.

**GI**  Just fruit juices and sherbert.

**MICKEY**  Probably why there's not much kick to it. Greyhound gotta flat so they were passing out some beverages, calm us down, with the delay, whatnot. But I been on the wagon since, well, for just forever, seems.

**GI**  You look good.

**MICKEY**  How old's this girl?

**GI**  I think twenty-three.

**MICKEY**  Same as Stef. But she don't speak English?

**GI**  She's just in the country a few months.

**MICKEY**  Stefan speaking Japanese now?

**GI**  He's actually picked up a few phrases.

**MICKEY**  Guess he'd have to, to get her to the altar. Or whatever that is.

**GI**  It's just a little . . . place for Buddha.

**MICKEY**  Any picture I've seen a Buddha suggests he's gonna need a bigger place to sit. This girl pregnant?

**GI**  Uh—

**MICKEY**  Just, so quick and all.

**GI**  No. She needs her green card.

**MICKEY**  Ah. She needs—

**GI**  She wants to be a decorator.

**MICKEY**  Decorated this place with the sliding walls?

**GI**  They're rice panels, made of paper.

**MICKEY**  Yeah, I noticed when I put my hand through one. Green card, huh? Stef getting paid for this?

**GI**  No. Stef's doing it for Shuji—her brother. Who taught Stef's Buddhist class. That's how they—the sister has to move in with Stef and Shuji, so it looks legal and all.

**MICKEY**   Well, you gotta live with the girl you marry, it's part of the deal.

**GI**   Mick, Stefan likes the brother.

**MICKEY**   Guess he'd have to, what with the brother moving in with them and all.

**GI**   No, the sister is moving—

**MICKEY**   That some kind of Japanese thing when women first get married? A family member has to live with her?

**GI**   No, he—Stefan really likes the brother and he's marrying the sister as a favor. This party's more on accounta how much Stefan really likes the brother. It's an arrangement.

**MICKEY**   Huh.

**GI**   It's a different kind of arrangement.

**MICKEY**   That business still going on?

**GI**   Seems, yeah.

**MICKEY**   Thought it was a phase, that kid from the summer theater.

**GI**   Well.

**MICKEY**   That big, polite, hairy kid.

**GI**   I don't think it's a phase.

**MICKEY**   But that girl with the, you know, that bolt through her nose?

**GI**   That was a nose ring.

**MICKEY**   Was attached to her nose.

**GI**  She was just a friend. They all got earrings that year before the holidays to outrage their parents. She really wanted to upset hers, I guess. (*beat*) Think he looks under the weather?

**MICKEY**  Nah, kids his age don't sleep.

**GI**  Just all this stuff you hear.

**MICKEY**  When I was his age—forget it. Drinking! Hoho! Having fun—

**GI**  It's just—I read stuff.

**MICKEY**  'Sides, you put a spell on him. Spell on me too. (*beat*) Lookit, you were always on me about doing something. And I been doing all kinda things to change. The typewriting, the night school. After years of big steel beams I'm pushing my hands on computer keys. Things I can't even do, I been telling myself I could do 'em. Been knocking off the bottle, Gi. So hard, Gi, knocking off the bottle.

**GI**  I know.

**MICKEY**  For so goddam long alone.

*Jesse enters.*

**JESSE**  Mick.

**MICKEY**  Jesse. How's it going?

**JESSE**  Fine. (*beat*) Your mother?

**MICKEY**  Ah, you know. Still kicking. (*beat*) Bake shop?

**GI**  The bake shop closed, Mick.

**JESSE**  I think they'd like to get started.

**MICKEY**   What, business bad, Jesse?

**JESSE**   I couldn't get a loan.

**GI**   But we're not going into the whole—

**JESSE**   No, no. (*to Gi*) You coming?

**GI**   Uh, we—

**MICKEY**   We haven't—the two of us need a few minutes.

**JESSE**   You do?

**MICKEY**   Yeah, to talk. Yeah, we do. What, that's not okay?

**GI**   Okay, we can all get along for one evening.

**MICKEY**   Hey, I'm getting along just fine.

**JESSE**   She's got this idea everyone gets along, or should.

**GI**   It's a party.

**JESSE**   This idea stuck in her head.

**MICKEY**   Ah, but people, you know, say one thing—then do another. You know, you turn your back and—just can't trust them.

**JESSE**   Not for real.

**MICKEY**   Not for long.

**JESSE** (*to Gi*)   Are you coming?

**MICKEY** (*to Gi*)   Where's your ring? It's your ring, I gave it to you—?

**GI**   I'm going back in.

**MICKEY** (*beat*)   Tell that Japanese girl she's got good taste in in-laws!

94

**GI**   Not gonna tell her anything. She's smart. She knows what she wants and she's getting it when she's young, which is nice I think.

**MICKEY**   Yeah, well, that's the Japanese all over. Right, Jesse?

**JESSE**   How you figure that, Mick?

**GI**   That's it.

**JESSE**   Nah, let's actually stay a minute and hear how your husband figures that.

**MICKEY**   "Her husband" is right.

**GI**   Please, they can hear.

**MICKEY**   The Japanese feel ripped off, you know, by the West. So they gotta come and buy the whole thing away from us. 'Cause they feel gypped outta what's theirs.

**GI**   Don't.

**MICKEY**   You watch, they'll buy the whole thing if we're not looking. And then they'll put their men in jobs we should rightly have.

**GI**   Don't do this.

**MICKEY**   We just gotta stand up for what's ours.

**JESSE**   You mean "yours."

**MICKEY**   And that is exactly why—

**GI**   They're watching.

**MICKEY**   That's exactly why I always thought you should have your shop where there's more your kinda—

**JESSE**   My kinda—?

**GI**  Let's not start with all that—

**MICKEY**  'Cause down south—now there's your market.

**GI**  He doesn't mean that.

**MICKEY**  People see something looks familiar, they buy it right up. But if they see something unfamiliar, say something—

**JESSE**  Black.

**MICKEY**  Joker!

**GI**  Please, not here.

**MICKEY**  Nah, but's true! Down south you got people more familiar to you.

**JESSE**  You mean black people.

**MICKEY**  People you grew up with. Myself, never ventured far and, well's held me in good stead. You know what I'm saying, Jesse?

**JESSE**  Saying—what I think you're saying is—

**MICKEY**  That's all I'm saying, Jesse.

**GI**  He's not saying anything.

**JESSE**  No, let me get this straight now. Everybody should stay where they come from, everybody should stay with their "kind," everybody should be—look at me!

**MICKEY**  (*to Jesse*)  Nothing more to you!

**GI**  Stop.

**JESSE**  Should be happy with what they start with?

**MICKEY** (*to Jesse*)  No.

**JESSE**  And stay in their "place"?

**MICKEY**  No!

**GI**  He's not saying that!

**JESSE**  Well, that's wrong.

**GI**  Please!

**JESSE**  That is simply wrong!

**GI**  Mick?

**JESSE**  Then what is he saying?

**GI** (*to Jesse*)  Don't.

**JESSE**  What is he possibly saying!

**MICKEY** (*to Gi*)  I'm saying EVERYTHING I BEEN DOING I BEEN DOING IT FOR YOU!

*The party chatter goes quiet.*

**GI** (*beat*)  But everything's changing, Mick.

**JESSE**  Gi?

**GI**  Whole world's changing. Look at us. Look in that room. (*talking to party*) Don't worry, it's just us old folks! We'll be right in. Please—everyone looks so nice. (*sounds of the party resume*) Whole world's . . . changed. Who'da thought? Who'da ever thought?

*Gi goes off. Jesse goes off. Mickey finally goes off. Mickey reenters holding flowers and Mair's travel bag. Gi reenters from the house carrying a small cardboard box. They meet on their front lawn. It is two years later.*

**GI**   Just waiting for the movers to finish loading the truck, so it's lucky you caught me. (*puts box down*) So—there's what's left of yours.

**MICKEY**   S'lot.

**GI**   Not that much after all.

**MICKEY**   Nuh, sure. (*offers flowers*) Uh—she had a vase in her room, so—

*Gi takes the flowers.*

**MICKEY** (*cont.*)   Place looks good.

**GI**   Finally got painted after the last squirrel moved out. How's the job?

**MICKEY**   Data entry still. Ain't exactly the welding. Steady check though, benefits.

**GI**   Good.

**MICKEY**   Supervisor's a kid half my age.

**GI**   Oh—Kid Mingey quit the baby business. Insurance was too high. So he's retired and he bought the Exxon. He makes them wash the windows when you pull up. Sorta jump out at you and throw a bucket of water over the window real quick like an amusement park ride. 'Course it costs more.

**MICKEY**   Worth it?

**GI**   This neighborhood?

**MICKEY**   Nuh, yeah, sure.

**GI**   Nice when we moved here.

**MICKEY**   Still gotta good price.

**GI**  Better than expected. Even with the railroad running the new line through. (*beat*) Got a letter from Jesse. From Alabama.

**MICKEY**  Huh.

**GI**  Yeah. His job is he looks for fires. With the police. In helicopters. Almost two years now. He sits in a helicopter and zooms over the tops of trees looking for just any kind of orange glow. Apparently he does that all day.

**MICKEY**  Guess he packs a lunch.

**GI**  He'd have to, can you imagine? (*regarding Mair's bag*) It was peaceful?

**MICKEY**  Just this plug in a socket. Next to her police radio plug. Like any plug you see. She was in and out.

**GI**  Did you tell her about the valances?

**MICKEY**  Forgot.

**GI**  The young couple was really impressed with the valances. They're in style again.

**MICKEY**  Hurt my hand the way she was holding it, but then, you know.

**GI**  Uh-huh.

**MICKEY**  Open the bag.

*Gi opens the bag.*

**GI**  Nothing.

**MICKEY**  How 'bout it. All this time thinking there was something worth something inside.

**GI**  Maybe someone took it out.

**MICKEY**  Nah, she told me right before—before, you know. She told me to open it. But I didn't till I was outta the room. Imagine holding on to something with nothing inside. That's nothing to end up with. (*beat*) Don't feel like a kid anymore.

**GI**  I'll give it to Stef. He loves old things. (*beat*) Shuji called.

**MICKEY**  How 'bout it.

**GI**  Wants to make sure I'm going up there for Thanksgiving this year.

**MICKEY**  That's six months off.

**GI**  Stef likes to plan lately. (*beat*) They have everyone over to their loft and they make a vegetarian turkey out of . . . ah . . . oh . . . soy products. So that's beans, I guess. And they stuff it with chick peas they mush up. So it's a big bean and chick-pea thing.

**MICKEY**  Guess you can eat the potatoes.

**GI**  'Course on Thanksgiving.

**MICKEY**  And should be greens and such.

**GI**  Just hope no one asks me to pass the beets.

**MICKEY**  You always had a nice meal. Coordinating it all— that's hard.

**GI**  Stef and Shuji make a meal for thirty people.

**MICKEY**  Boy's strong.

**GI**  He takes a lot of naps apparently.

**MICKEY**  That's good.

**GI**  And they don't chant or anything, and I don't think he's Buddhist anymore 'cause they don't thank Buddha or anything, they just kind of send up energy to the sky.

**MICKEY**  Shoulda sent him to public school, saved the money.

**GI**  Who'da thought?

**MICKEY**  You raised him to be strong.

**GI**  (*beat*)  You want anything?

**MICKEY**  Nuh.

**GI**  Some root beer? Got some sitting in there for the movers.

**MICKEY**  Fine, nuh.

**GI**  You want it, you're just not saying it. (*she goes into the house and calls from off*) The little cards I'm doing are in all the shops. A man came back a month or so ago, a distributor and I had them laying out, and he bought them. The *idea* he bought.

**MICKEY**  How 'bout it.

**GI**  And a factory makes them now. So they're all over in the stores and people call me up. (*reenters with root beer*) They really are communicating with people all over the place. And then there's money too—for the first time. And I'm going to Paris.

**MICKEY**  That's great, Gi.

**GI**  Paris, France, Mick. A little trip. (*beat*) The cards have little animals on them. Maybe I showed you one once?

**MICKEY**  Don't think so.

**GI**   There're little sayings on them some other person writes like: "On your birthday, have a bear of a time." That's not a good one. There's one I like that says: "Don't be chicken, give me a call sometime." Guess that's not so hot either. They wanted to make one with squirrels and I—I put my foot down. I went, went, "No squirrels! You should see what they did to our roof."

**MICKEY**   You tell people something like that and they look at you like you got two heads!

**GI**   They think you're crazy. But apparently the cards're "moving." That's what they say, "moving." Guess that means they're going places. So many people and me are connected. (*beat*) I still don't have any girlfriends. Most women have girlfriends.

**MICKEY**   Busy s'all.

**GI**   I'da liked a grandchild. I'd like that for Stef. 'Cause there's still time. And today people have all kinds of options, like adopting and, well, just all kinds of options about anything you and me never even . . . especially women. Lookit what she's doing in the White House, right?

**MICKEY**   (*touching her hair*)   What's this?

**GI**   It's my hair.

**MICKEY**   But it's silver.

**GI**   It's a rinse. My hairdresser said if I kept dyeing it, then it'd fall out eventually, imagine? So he just rinses it out with a little color so there's silver coming through.

**MICKEY**   Just a little.

**GI**   I'm fifty-three.

**MICKEY**   S'nuthin.

**GI**   Coulda gone bald! (*beat*) We're simple people. We wanted simple—

**MICKEY**   Shh.

**GI** (*beat*)   The couple who's moving in's from Sri Lanka. She said they could make use of the rec room. Didn't ask her for what. I told her to go ahead and try, we never knew what the hell to do with it.

**MICKEY**   Ah you know, they get ideas.

**GI**   Uh-huh.

**MICKEY**   New-marrieds have all kindsa ideas 'bout a new place.

**GI**   They aren't even married.

**MICKEY**   Kids today, right?

**GI**   No one gets married anymore anyway. Think you get married as like an insurance thing that you hope there's gonna be someone at the end. Think it's the cruelest thing we do to people. But's hard not to be cruel so much of the time. Should just marry them 'cause they bother us less than most people.

**MICKEY**   Probably won't reco'nize the place if we ever drive by.

**GI**   New train won't even stop here, express only, city to city. The house'll just be like a blurry speck when you go by. No one'd even know anyone lived here they'd be going by so fast. I'm always wondering what's the hurry. What's the hurry?

**MICKEY**   Always a bus man myself.

**GI**  Just the house was just too big for just me.

**MICKEY**  Always felt bad it was small.

**GI**  It was. Now it's too big.

*The sound of a truck's engine is heard nearby.*

**MICKEY**  Guess the movers are done.

**GI**  Yes.

**MICKEY**  Look. (*pointing*) Rhododendron got their flowers.

**GI**  Lining the walk.

**MICKEY**  Spring is what.

**GI**  We planted them.

**MICKEY**  Spring's what it is.

**GI**  Who'da even noticed? All that's been going on.

*Lights fade. End of Play.*

# MINUTES FROM
# THE BLUE ROUTE

for Peter, who found his home

*Minutes from the Blue Route* was produced by Atlantic Theater Company (Neil Pepe, Artistic Director; Hillary Hinkle, Managing Director) in New York City on January 16, 1997. The play was directed by David Warren. The scenery was designed by Derek McLane, the costumes by Mark Wedland, the lighting by Donald Holder, and the music and sound by John Gromada. The stage manager was Janet Takami. The cast was:

| | |
|---|---|
| **OLDEST** | Matt McGrath |
| **MOTHER** | Elizabeth Franz |
| **FATHER** | Stephen Mendillo |
| **YOUNGEST** | Catherine Kellner |

The play takes place in a suburban home, on a Labor Day weekend right before an election.

*Minutes From The Blue Route* was originaly produced by New York Stage and Film Company (Mark Linn-Baker, Max Mayer, Leslie Airting, Producing Directors; Peter Manning, Producer) in Poughkeepsie, New York, in July, 1995. It was directed by David Warren; the set design was by Derek McLane; the costume design was by Teresa Snider-Stein; the lighting design was by Donald Holder; the original music and sound design were by John Gromada; and the production stage manager was Janet Takami. The cast was as follows:

| | |
|---|---|
| **OLDEST** | Matt McGrath |
| **MOTHER** | Dana Ivey |
| **FATHER** | Jack Davidson |
| **YOUNGEST** | Wendy Hoopes |

It is something strictly American to conceive a space that is so filled with moving.

—Gertrude Stein,
*The Making of Americans*

# ACT ONE

MOTHER, *wearing rubber gloves, glasses around her neck, and an apron over her clothes, stands behind a few cardboard boxes.* OLDEST *has just come in the door. It is 5:00 P.M. on a Friday.*

**OLDEST**   I can't stay long.

**MOTHER**   No, no, we know. You're early—?

**OLDEST**   I took a cab from the station.

**MOTHER**   You spent money on a cab from the station?

**OLDEST**   I actually spent money on a cab from the station.

**MOTHER**   We were waiting for a call—did you eat?

**OLDEST**   Yeah, sure.

**MOTHER**   Your father ate all morning. Older he gets, more he eats.

**OLDEST**   On the train I ate.

**MOTHER**   He's fifty-eight! Fat. I'm near that. Not so fat. You'll see, all around here. (*her stomach*) I've been trying to get him to Jazzercise. (*beat*) You ate train food? 'Cause we were gonna go 'round the, up the farmer's market if it's still open—? They've got pasta dishes in, wrapped up, for the microwave.

**OLDEST**   I can't even think about—

**MOTHER**   Fettucini?

**OLDEST**   Food now, no.

**MOTHER**   Maybe later. You look good.

**OLDEST**  I can't stay long.

**MOTHER**  Your face does.

**OLDEST**  There's all this stuff with the new job.

**MOTHER**  Just a talk, she'll be back soon. All grown up. That's what she thinks. College is grown up. You were grown up, that age.

**OLDEST**  I was in a hurry.

**MOTHER**  You were always—

**OLDEST**  I was mature.

**MOTHER**  Mature, for your age, smoking, out all night, fancy friends. Older ones. Books by strange authors. You had a look in your eyes like an old man. We have pictures of it.

**OLDEST**  (*pointing to boxes*)  You need help?

**MOTHER**  Oh, throwing out things, no. Consolidating, throwing out. (*closes a box*) She gets off at four. This job goes to four. Full-time now, but they accommodate her for school. They hold her job. If she goes back. Just a little talk.

**OLDEST**  I know what to say.

**MOTHER**  Say "school is important." And don't get into a whole rigamarole. Just say school is—

**OLDEST**  School is important.

**MOTHER**  It is. (*beat*) They're accommodating this pregnant woman she's working with. So when it looked like they weren't gonna accommodate your sister, they were gonna give her trouble with school, holding her job this last year, she made a stink to the management. Your sister gets difficult. (*beat*) 'Cause, you know, half the store is part-time—they just thought, because she was young, maybe she should want overtime. She's got more energy is the thinking. 'Cause I know from my job we're always asking the young people to, you know, lift something, move things, work the holidays, work around pregnant people. That's a lot!

**OLDEST**  It is.

**MOTHER**  It is.

**OLDEST**  I know.

**MOTHER**  No, I know you know. So she got difficult. But the whole world's full-time now. Everybody's working, everybody's full-time. It's the age we live in. (*beat*) You look good.

**OLDEST**  It hasn't been that long.

**MOTHER**  Your face, your body.

**OLDEST**  Eight months?

**MOTHER**  Your father and I've been meaning to get up, but with your schedule, which is—who knows how you do it!

**OLDEST**  I take a lot of speed.

**MOTHER**  (*smiles*)  Well, who knows how. One thing and another and all our weddings—there's one every week practically. Everybody's children feel the need to, uh, couple off.

**OLDEST**  In March you were up.

**MOTHER**  Right, March, sure. The Breznian boy's getting married tomorrow. Remember Tommy?

**OLDEST**  No.

**MOTHER**  With the forehead? No?

**OLDEST**  Mmm . . . ?

**MOTHER**  To a woman accountant. And that's what he does. They met at their same firm. That's tomorrow's wedding.

**OLDEST**  You'll have to come up when—

**MOTHER**  Sometime.

**OLDEST**  I guess when people stop getting married.

**MOTHER**  (*smiles*)  Oh, you think no one does anymore, but they just do it later. Thirty, forty. Your father likes it though—free food. Wait'll you see! (*makes fat face*) Next month maybe. See the leaves. Visit, see the leaves, get lunch, shop a little.

**OLDEST**  No one I know's married.

**MOTHER**  Monica's married, you know her.

**OLDEST**  She's—they were together forever, that's a whole complicated—

**MOTHER**  She have her baby?

**OLDEST**  Yeah. Ten months! Ow. They induced it.

**MOTHER**  Induced, huh. Sometimes they have to.

**OLDEST**  (*beat*)  Next month might be tricky. For visiting.

**MOTHER**  Oh—

**OLDEST**  And I can only stay the night 'cause I've got to open the shop tomorrow. I'll have to get up early so I need an alarm clock.

**MOTHER**  You're working at a shop?

112

**OLDEST** Between things.

**MOTHER** There's an alarm clock in a box here . . . (*she finds it*) We'll set it by the couch.

**OLDEST** I'd stay longer.

**MOTHER** This is nice, though.

**OLDEST** There's all these things.

**MOTHER** No, no.

**OLDEST** Things need doing.

**MOTHER** (*taking boxes off the couch*)  You have to sleep on the couch which is rotten, I know, but your room's where we keep things now. Sweaters, for winter. Mothballs. Stinks. There's potpourri tucked places, little bags your aunt made, but it doesn't help. (*re: couch*) And this doesn't pull out, but—

**OLDEST** No, fine, it's just everyone's gone this weekend for some reason and I got elected to open the shop every day and—

**MOTHER** Well, you do that a little, you open that shop, your boss sees you're doing that—

**OLDEST** It's a—no.

**MOTHER** —he gets to like you—

**OLDEST** It's an in-the-meantime job. No. Jonathan set me up between things and things're slow, for some reason it's really slow. Kids don't want magicians or something. And Jonathan—you remember him? The hair?

**MOTHER** Oh, yeah.

**OLDEST** He had this job opening at this tchotchke shop— uh—he owns this shop? Little tchotchkes for Christmas.

MOTHER   Jonathan with the hair, sure.

OLDEST   So, yeah, so he's just opened this shop for Christmas things.

MOTHER   It's September.

OLDEST   Well—it's mostly Christmas, there's some other stuff until then.

MOTHER   Ah.

OLDEST   There's like turkey stuff. And, um, decorative Pilgrims. And little skulls, with, like, candles in them, in their skulls—

MOTHER   Halloween.

OLDEST   Halloween stuff, other holidays. They're branching out.

MOTHER   Huh, that's—

OLDEST   But mostly it's Christmas. That's the bulk of the . . . business.

MOTHER   Well, sure—

OLDEST   Sure, uh, so that's his store and then in January I'll probably go out to L.A.

MOTHER   Benefits?

OLDEST   Group plan.

MOTHER   Good.

OLDEST   We've all joined it and I can stay on it after I leave the job.

MOTHER   Good, group plan, very good.

**OLDEST**  Which should be January, uh, when I'll maybe move to L.A.

**MOTHER**  L.A.?

**OLDEST**  Apparently kids want magicians there. Or so he says. Jonathan. That's where he's flying—(*looks at watch*) about now, as a matter of fact. Opening another shop. L.A., fake snow, snow you . . . spray on surfaces. Nothing's definite.

**MOTHER**  Then—this is nice.

**OLDEST**  The couch is completely fine.

**MOTHER**  Do the thing with the quarter I like.

*Oldest produces a quarter from behind her ear. Mother giggles and applauds. A moment passes.*

**OLDEST**  What?

**MOTHER**  I'm just looking at you. I haven't seen you in a while.

**OLDEST**  Six months is nothing.

**MOTHER**  (*beat*)  I bet I know who you're voting for. Soon, a new election, a chance to change things, how 'bout that? Keep some people, dump some others. (*beat*) She'll be home any minute, then you can talk. (*starts to go*) Just promise me we won't get into a whole rigamarole.

**OLDEST**  No . . . rigamarole.

**MOTHER**  And don't ask your father who he's voting for, we're not—just don't. Every four years I threaten divorce. (*beat*) You know, just let me call him before he leaves work. The market's on his way. We can always freeze it, then microwave it later. That's one of the good things about the age we live in.

*Mother sits on sofa, putting things in a box.* FATHER *enters with a newspaper and sits in a chair. Oldest sits next to Mother and picks up a newspaper. It is 10:00 P.M. that evening.*

**OLDEST**   Where is she?

**MOTHER**   She does overtime sometimes.

**OLDEST**   She doesn't call when she does overtime?

**MOTHER**   They get busy and they're too busy and they can't reach the phone. If she's at the register.

**FATHER** (*beat*)   You got the B section, boy?

**OLDEST**   Yesterday's.

**MOTHER**   If she's at the register she literally cannot reach to the phone.

**OLDEST** (*handing over paper*)   No, today's.

**MOTHER**   I've seen the setup.

**FATHER** (*beat*)   How 'bout those pasta meals?

**OLDEST**   Oh, yeah.

**MOTHER**   They did it to keep them from gabbing.

**FATHER**   They've changed our lives.

**MOTHER**   Gab, gab, gab on the phone.

**FATHER**   Plus the microwave, years now.

**MOTHER**   So they put the phone far away from their reach. So they can't call their mothers when they're late. (*to Father*) He doesn't believe in microwaves.

**FATHER**   What's there to believe or not?

**OLDEST**  The fettucini was really . . . tasty. Jonathan and I go to this place—

**FATHER**  He looks good, doesn't he?

**MOTHER**  He's in a group plan.

**FATHER**  That's good.

**MOTHER**  From the shop that even takes care of his teeth.

**OLDEST**  This little pasta store is right near me.

**FATHER**  Ours doesn't do that. This last one. (*taps teeth*) But we've got a dentist with reasonable rates.

**OLDEST**  There's a little pasta store opened in my neighborhood that makes fresh . . . fettucini.

**MOTHER**  His friend with the hair.

**FATHER**  Oh, yeah.

**MOTHER**  With the shop where he works?

**FATHER**  Christmas stuff.

**OLDEST**  It's not just . . . well, it's mostly Christmas. (*beat*) Yeah, having the dentist covered is . . . great. It really is.

**FATHER**  And your mother's got big teeth—so reasonable rates—if we paid per tooth size! Phew!

**OLDEST**  A lot of my friends don't even have insurance, so I know, you know, how lucky it is.

**MOTHER**  They didn't cover his caps.

**OLDEST**  No, that's cosmetic. I mean, we live in a country—

**FATHER**  Caps? For what?

**MOTHER**  His teeth were getting yellow.

**OLDEST**  Coffee.

**MOTHER**  Magicians can't have yellow teeth.

**OLDEST**  You realize we live in the only civilized country—

**MOTHER**  He quit the cigarettes.

**FATHER**  Coffee's no good.

**OLDEST**  I'm just lucky I lucked into a job that covers everything during a time when, when nothing's covered. For so many people.

**FATHER**  (*beat*)  Good, good. Who you voting for?

**MOTHER**  We're not getting into that. Please.

**FATHER**  Look, when she gets here? Don't jump down her throat. You know how she gets, she's a hardhead.

**MOTHER**  (*to Oldest*)  Everyone's a "hardhead."

**OLDEST**  I wouldn't jump down her—

**FATHER**  Just tell her outright you think it's a good idea to stay in college.

**OLDEST**  When have I—?

**MOTHER**  She's got a whole scholarship.

**FATHER**  A full scholarship, room, board, tuition, books.

**MOTHER**  A stipend.

**FATHER**  A stipend does not grow on trees. Use of a car, a communal car.

**OLDEST**  Okay.

**MOTHER**  They have to sign it out.

**FATHER**   You don't get this offer all the time.

**MOTHER**   Or else someone might monopolize it.

**FATHER**   She stays in school one more year—

**MOTHER**   *If* she takes the intercession.

**OLDEST**   Okay.

**FATHER**   She takes the intercession, by next June she's out, she's making money. She's set and we don't have to—

**MOTHER**   —worry about her. No worries.

**OLDEST**   Okay, while I'm here, if we could all do me the courtesy, okay, of not thinking I would jump down anyone's throat. Or get into a whole rigamarole.

**FATHER**   Fair enough.

**MOTHER** *(beat)*   She might not want to take the intercession. And that's her prerogative. X-session. And the stipend's the same during X-session. You know, and that's all if she goes back.

**FATHER**   We know you won't jump down her throat.

**OLDEST**   She gets a stipend?

**MOTHER**   That's very nice, isn't it?

**FATHER**   Those people make forty thou, starting salary. What I made when I started? When Bud set me up? We had that little company, paring knives, I don't know—your sister? Forty thou, easy.

**OLDEST**   How much of a stipend?

**FATHER**   Big.

**MOTHER**   And she's been approached already.

**FATHER**  She's been approached by companies already, yes she has.

**MOTHER**  Big ones, out of state.

**FATHER**  Just talk some sense into her. She's a hardhead like your mother.

**MOTHER**  I'm a "hardhead," she's a "hardhead," Beth Ann Phelan at work is a "hardhead"—

**OLDEST**  I can't stay an extra day, really! Jonathan's flying, he's in the air now, somewhere above us, and there's only the two of us who have keys to the shop—and, well, Claudio. But Claudio's got a share at the beach and his machine's always on which drives everyone nuts if you need him 'cause there's no getting at him. (*beat*) So I was elected so I have to open. So I can't not go back. If she doesn't come home.

**FATHER**  (*beat*)  She'll come home. It's only—what?

**MOTHER**  (*looking at her watch*)  Mine says ten.

**OLDEST**  Just so we all know.

**FATHER**  (*looking at his watch*)  Mine says ten-oh-six.

**OLDEST**  I should turn in.

*Oldest starts to go.*

**MOTHER**  We're selling the house. (*beat*) We found a buyer. Fourteen months on the market, not a nibble—but out of nowhere.

**FATHER**  A bachelor.

**MOTHER**  What?

**FATHER**  Nothing, he's a bachelor.

**MOTHER**  Your father's always implying things.

**OLDEST**  Really, a buyer? I didn't—

**MOTHER**  Fourteen months!

**OLDEST**  I thought you'd given up—

**MOTHER**  No more mowing lawns—

**FATHER** (*to Oldest*)  No, no.

**MOTHER**  And empty rooms and hedges and flooding basements with no one to help. Your fat father with pails of water! Red from exertion. The wallpaper, twenty years old! Just a little apartment somewhere. Small. Manageable. Less dusting.

**FATHER**  We didn't give up.

**MOTHER**  We just kept hoping.

**OLDEST**  So the boxes . . . ?

**FATHER**  This is all just talk, until we go to contract.

**MOTHER** (*closing another box*)  I'm just consolidating. (*beat*) That's how they say it when everyone commits, "go to contract." (*beat*) Your father might have to retire early.

**FATHER**  Nobody said that yet.

**MOTHER**  And to keep up a house.

**OLDEST**  Why early?

**MOTHER**  His company is doing something.

**FATHER**  Reconfiguring—

**MOTHER**  Downsizing. Nobody wants so many planes anymore.

**FATHER**   But nobody's come out and actually—

**MOTHER**   It's been scary.

**FATHER**   It's all talk.

**MOTHER**   And to keep a house when you don't want worries—

**OLDEST**   What worries?

**MOTHER**   And with the money we spend just on electricity we could rent an apartment—

**OLDEST**   What worries?

**FATHER**   Just let's leave the future what it is.

**MOTHER**   We just have to work out the logistics.

**FATHER**   Nobody's worried.

**OLDEST**   Don't worry about me, if that's the worry.

**MOTHER**   It's the business with your sister. If she doesn't go back to school—

**FATHER**   She'll go back.

**MOTHER**   There wasn't even a question until we got a buyer, then all of a sudden—

**FATHER**   She'll come 'round.

**MOTHER**   It's the business with the accident, which got her scared.

**FATHER**   He'll talk to her.

**MOTHER**   Her classes start next week.

**FATHER**   She'll go back.

**MOTHER**   So if she doesn't go back to school—she'd stay here. And since the accident—

**FATHER**   She's just—

**MOTHER**   She's apprehensive. She hardly leaves the house. We can't kick her out. So she'd stay. We'd have to say no to this buyer.

**OLDEST** (*to Father*)   Can you retire?

**MOTHER**   And in this market—

**FATHER**   No one's retiring.

**MOTHER**   To get a buyer when we haven't saved a dime.

**FATHER**   That's a trend.

**MOTHER**   What with things so tight, college for you—

**FATHER**   I'm not part of that trend.

**MOTHER**   All that lost on Bud's lousy advice, your fat father's back. Fourteen months and nothing. And in this market—

**FATHER**   People still want planes.

**OLDEST**   You haven't . . . planned?

**FATHER**   We planned and planned.

**MOTHER**   Things happen. (*beat*) What's this world coming to when people don't need planes or magic?

**FATHER**   We just can't go to contract until your sister's persuaded.

**MOTHER**   On Tuesday we could go to contract. And it's Friday, so—

**FATHER**   We're close.

**MOTHER**   We're close. That's the only worry.

**OLDEST**   So you're packing.

**MOTHER**   Hopefully. (*beat*) There's such a—a little window. Of opportunity. And you've got to—to get through it, hopefully. If she doesn't go back to school—

**FATHER**   She'll go back, she's in a sorority! (*to Oldest*) How long can you stay?

**OLDEST**   Not long.

**MOTHER**   Not long.

**OLDEST**   Just the night.

**FATHER** (*to Mother*)   Did you show him that book you found?

**MOTHER**   This bible you made.

**FATHER**   You drew this whole bible.

**MOTHER**   On the front it says "written by" and then there's a colon and then the word "God."

**FATHER**   Written by God!

**MOTHER**   You got an A. It's packed somewhere.

**FATHER**   Just the night?

**OLDEST**   I'd stay longer—

**MOTHER**   He's got things.

**FATHER**   We all do.

**OLDEST**   I would, you know. I would.

*Father and Mother go back to the newspaper.*

**FATHER**   You think he's the right candidate but I never trusted his look.

**MOTHER**   Oh, lookit here, it says they're redeveloping the waterfront!

**OLDEST**   Huh.

**MOTHER** (*to Oldest*)   And you like boats!

*Mother and Father go upstairs. Oldest falls asleep on the couch with the alarm clock set on the floor.* YOUNGEST *comes in from outside. It is 6:00 A.M., Saturday, the next morning.*

**YOUNGEST**   What're you doing here?

**OLDEST**   What time is it?

**YOUNGEST** (*beat*)   Are you here to talk to me? Did they get you here to talk to me?

**OLDEST**   They paid for the train.

**YOUNGEST**   Oh, God, and you came.

**OLDEST**   I had a day free.

**YOUNGEST**   And you came.

**OLDEST**   I haven't been home in—

**YOUNGEST**   I'm not going back. Those courses!

**OLDEST**   What time is it?

**YOUNGEST**   I don't want to hear a lecture from you about time.

**OLDEST**   No, no.

**YOUNGEST**   I'm almost twenty-two, if I come in late—

**OLDEST**   No, I just—

**YOUNGEST**  Three years of business, business courses—I know retail! I'm currently doing retail. So what are courses for? (*sneezes*) Allergies. And you're supposed to, what, talk to me?

**OLDEST**  I had a day free.

**YOUNGEST**  You look like shit.

**OLDEST**  It's—something fucking something A.M.!

**YOUNGEST**  It's six.

**OLDEST**  Excuse me, Miss Waltzing-in-here—

**YOUNGEST**  It's six, so it's six.

**OLDEST**  Waltzing in here at dawn—

**YOUNGEST**  He doesn't get off till two. A guy! But I'm allowed to hang out in the lounge. Where he works there's a lounge the girlfriends hang out in and stare at each other 'cause we all dated the same people like ten years ago. Then we stopped for breakfast. He's half Greek and half Hawaiian. (*looking upstairs*) They don't care. I don't know anyone who cares anymore. I've known him forever, but all of a sudden, this total guy! (*beat*) You don't live here, don't start in about time! (*sneezes*) Mold allergies. The basement flooded and there's mold clinging to carpeting. (*she puts her head in her brother's lap*) His days are free but then I'm on this day shift. (*dozing*) I have to get up . . . I have to get up soon. Look at this room . . . I'm almost asleep. How many times have we seen this room almost asleep? (*beat*) And they have a buyer!

**OLDEST**  Yes.

**YOUNGEST**  This huge homo! They think he's single. (*beat*) Are you single?

126

**OLDEST**   You know, between his job and the way things are going so slow for me—

**YOUNGEST**   Uh-huh.

**OLDEST**   And he's always flying everywhere.

**YOUNGEST**   Jonathan.

**OLDEST**   Right, and I've got to stay where the work is, which is, you know—

**YOUNGEST**   Uh-huh.

**OLDEST**   —lately more and more really nowhere.

**YOUNGEST**   I'll come up. I'll come up and take care of you!

**OLDEST**   In January I'm going out. L.A. Probably. He wants to make it work. And he's got this house. To live in. And if both the stores go well—he's got these Christmas stores—not just Christmas but all kinds of holiday tchotchkes. And so yeah, if the stores take off year-round there's not so much travel. So we'd live in the house he's got. If I decided.

**YOUNGEST**   Cha-kas—?

**OLDEST**   It's Jewish for little . . . stupid something—Yiddish, Yiddish, he'd kill me.

**YOUNGEST**   I'll make my store transfer me!

**OLDEST**   No, I'm going out.

**YOUNGEST**   We're in malls all over now!

**OLDEST**   February, latest.

**YOUNGEST**   I'll come up.

**OLDEST**   And I've got all these connections now—

**YOUNGEST**   But I like this house.

**OLDEST**   Connections across the country. From doing magic all over. There's all these people everywhere between him and here and they've all practically all said stay with us, whenever.

**YOUNGEST**   This house.

**OLDEST**   So I have a choice. Between Jonathan's house and other houses.

**YOUNGEST**   This house! I know where everything is.

**OLDEST**   And what good're connections across a huge—

**YOUNGEST**   Everything.

**OLDEST**   —country if you don't—

**YOUNGEST**   Everything.

**OLDEST**   —you know, connect?

**YOUNGEST**   (*beat*)   One year's forever.

**OLDEST**   It is. (*beat*) No, it's nothing! Who's he kidding—we wouldn't last two days in the same house. I mean, just for instance, the rabbits? All the bunnies I pull from hats? I live with them. They're in cages in my apartment. He'd have to put up with . . . bunnies. Actually, he thinks they're cute. He named them. One bunny's named Jean Michel. Jonathan made him a beret. He thought he looked French. He even cleans the cages 'cause I'm not supposed to handle—there's stuff in the bunny poop you shouldn't go near when you're . . .

**YOUNGEST**   You don't look bad. (*sneezes*) They said it's the highest mold spore count in years this week which really, really sucks! (*beat*) I want to travel and, you know, I want to mix it up and, all that, you know—get a job, quit it, get a job, quit it—stuff you did! All that stuff. They can transfer me anywhere! (*beat*) You're not gonna go out, he's been asking you forever.

*Mother comes downstairs in her bathrobe.*

**MOTHER**   Anyone hungry?

**YOUNGEST**   It didn't work. This bit, him coming home?

**MOTHER**   (*long beat*)   I'll make eggs if anyone's hungry.

**OLDEST**   (*looks at his watch*)   I won't have time for food.

**MOTHER**   You'll eat—you'll stay here and eat. (*beat*) Your father'll run out for cinnamon buns. (*Mother goes off to the kitchen.*)

**OLDEST**   Go the year. There's such a . . . such a little window—and when it's open . . .

**YOUNGEST**   What?

**OLDEST**   Opportunity . . . um . . .

*Father comes downstairs in his pajamas.*

**FATHER**   Everyone's up, that's a sign of something!

*Mother comes in from kitchen, whisking eggs in a bowl.*

**MOTHER**   (*to Oldest*) Someone else can open that shop! You call someone else to open that shop. It's nowhere near Christmas. (*to Father*) And you—run out for cinnamon buns right now!

*The alarm clock rings. Father and Oldest exit. Mother takes off her bathrobe. Underneath she wears a semi-formal dress. Youngest picks through the remains of cinnamon buns. It is now 10:00 A.M. Mother sits and begins to sort through the contents of one of the boxes.*

**MOTHER** (*beat*)  You can have your friend over, we don't bite.

**YOUNGEST**  He works nights.

**MOTHER** (*pulls a mug from a box*)  You want this?

**YOUNGEST**  No.

**MOTHER**  You can come to the wedding. Your name was on the invitation. It's casual, you could just throw something on. They have casual weddings, now they do. I'm just dressed like this because it was clean.

**YOUNGEST**  I've got work?

**MOTHER**  You're the same age as Tommy Breznian. He was in your grade school. His ashtray won over yours. Which set us all back. Well, it was rough going there a while.

**YOUNGEST**  It's kinda behind me.

**MOTHER**  Well, no, c'mon, I'm not—it just occurred to me. I'm not that far gone. (*beat*) He looks good.

**YOUNGEST**  He's good.

**MOTHER**  Well, yes.

**YOUNGEST**  Good people look good.

**MOTHER** (*pulls a stuffed animal from a box*)  This?

**YOUNGEST**  No. (*beat*) You know, all this elaborate—this—ucchh—I hate this whole—

**MOTHER**  I'm not—

**YOUNGEST**  This whole—

**MOTHER**  It's not—

**YOUNGEST**  Whatever, this little game—

**MOTHER**  He wanted to visit.

**YOUNGEST**  This business.

**MOTHER**  He did.

**YOUNGEST**  Oh, he didn't, you know, he just didn't. (*drawing in the air*) Here's his list—here's visiting us. (*she indicates the bottom of the list*) You wanted to see how he looked.

*She puts her head in her mother's lap.*

**MOTHER**  You're not feeling well?

**YOUNGEST**  Whatever.

**MOTHER**  In the bathroom?

**YOUNGEST**  We drank too much last night.

**MOTHER**  I thought you weren't.

**YOUNGEST**  Not for a while I wasn't. The sulfites, the wine.

**MOTHER**  The accident scared you.

**YOUNGEST**  It was an "aborted flight." (*beat*) He likes wine. But the sulfites destroy me every time.

**MOTHER**  And the mold spore count is through the roof.

**YOUNGEST**  It is! (*beat*) I'm okay with wine. (*beat*) Don't call it an "accident"! It went up, it came down. An accident is when you crash to a grisly death.

**MOTHER** (*beat*)  You're too old for my lap. The dress gets wrinkled. (*Youngest sits up*) I'm through with this one— everyone's seen it. They all go to the same—everyone should just have one big wedding like that cult. All the money everybody puts out. You could—you wouldn't want this dress? I always wanted a girl.

**YOUNGEST**  Well, you got one. (*beat*) Look, I'll invite him over if you don't ask questions.

**MOTHER**  What?

**YOUNGEST**  Questions, little questions. After dinner, one night, maybe.

**MOTHER**  What questions?

**YOUNGEST**  Maybe before his shift. (*beat*) All those little questions you ask.

**MOTHER**  (*beat*) You know, I have a life too! I have a life that has to be worked around too. I'm full-time at the job, I can't be full-time here. I would like him over, yes. But not if there's all these conditions.

**YOUNGEST**  We're not getting married.

**MOTHER**  Who said anything?

**YOUNGEST**  Okay.

**MOTHER**  Who said anything?

**YOUNGEST**  We're just—not.

**MOTHER**  (*takes a figurine from a box*) You don't want this?

**YOUNGEST**  I do want that, I said last week I do!

**MOTHER**  (*beat*) Your hair looks pretty, down like that.

**YOUNGEST**  Don't talk about my hair. Just—don't. (*beat*) The thing that really gets me is when I was fat nobody said I had pretty hair and now everybody says it all the time. It's the same hair, it's just on a less fatter face. (*beat*) Would you want to go halfway across the country to East Nowhere, all girls, freezing cold, business, business, business courses, three in a room—there's three girls until senior year, they're all taking the same courses, dating the same guys, synchronizing their cycles—and for what? To get out, to do retail, when I'm doing all aspects of retail now. And I've been promoted.

**MOTHER**   You're smarter than that.

**YOUNGEST**   I've been promoted twice over the summer.

**MOTHER**   Much, much smarter.

**YOUNGEST**   And no, God, I would not want to wear that dress ever. (*beat*) Each aspect of retail I know. I was voted "Best in Mall."

**MOTHER**   (*beat*)   A fine school, a full scholarship! People don't get those. (*beat*) We've got a buyer.

**YOUNGEST**   Can I take a shower?

**MOTHER**   I know your father told you. (*beat*) The dress was an idea! (*beat*) When your father's out of the bathroom you can take a shower.

**YOUNGEST**   And don't sneak and throw that figurine out.

**MOTHER**   (*beat*)   We didn't, all this time, we didn't—your father and I—so you could toss everything—

**YOUNGEST**   He's been in there forever!

**MOTHER**   My mother—when she was—I'm not going into this again.

**YOUNGEST**   You could kick me out.

**MOTHER**   After fourteen months of no one, nothing—!

**YOUNGEST**   Everyone I know's been kicked out, least twice.

**MOTHER**   You'll always have a home. That's not the question here. Huh? He's fifty-eight, I'm almost that. People live forever now. Years left, years. Try managing that. Another lifetime.

**YOUNGEST**   You're just scared.

**MOTHER**   When you're older and you see things—things happen. And if you're not prepared . . .

**YOUNGEST**   (*beat*)   I need a shower before work. (*beat*) He's been in there forever!

**MOTHER**   He's reading the paper. He likes that.

**YOUNGEST**   I thought you had a wedding.

**MOTHER**   I'm just ready, that's all!

*Youngest goes upstairs. Mother starts taping boxes shut. The phone rings. Oldest enters and picks up phone. It is noon.*

**OLDEST**   (*on phone*)   It's just today, there's a complication. Listen, a complication, listen. They're under the sink. Claudio can overnight them to you. I put them under the sink in a plastic bag, no. In felt-tip marker on the bag it says "Santa's Head." No, no, I know it says "Rudolph." Because the reindeer sleds were originally in the packing. But tell him under that in felt-tip marker it says—

**MOTHER**   Do you want me to leave?

**OLDEST**   (*shakes head no*)   The same packing, August at least. Just have Claudio call me when he gets there instead of you calling me on your cell and relaying to him—listen! Boxes in a big, Christmasy bag, he'll see them—they stick out. The sleds stick out of the boxes, no. They don't fit really but they're secure. They're more secure in the sled casing— the "Rudolph's Sled" casing.

134

**MOTHER**   I can leave.

**OLDEST**   (*shakes his head maybe*)   No, no, not now, okay. Yes, absolutely for tomorrow. (*lowering his voice*) Yes, "purple." Purple, purple. Remember "purple"? Our little purple thing? (*beat*) Exactly. Right. Purple here. Okay, when are you flying back? Well, I can't help that, Claudio will just have to grow up and put some clothes on and leave the beach. He's got a key, I made him one.

**MOTHER**   Ask him can you get a discount?

**OLDEST**   (*hangs up phone*)   Yes, Mother, I work there.

*Mother and Oldest go outside. The phone rings again. Father enters from upstairs, dressed for the wedding, and picks up the phone. It is 1:00 P.M.*

**FATHER**   Hey-ho. (*beat*) Hallarya? No, it's all going through, your bank's all over it. We were looking at, when we talked last, we were saying what—Tuesday? Tuesday since Monday—yeah Tuesday we'll talk, Monday's the holiday, right, so Tuesday we'll talk. Ah, yeah it's just there's a few things, bup-pa, you know, personal. We've been here coming on thirty years, twenty-some-odd years and there's a, my young kid, my girl—there's some question. (*beat*) No, not, it's we're needing, we're needing, we're needing time. One day, two. Two days. She's got "issues." Ah, well she's a hardhead. It's, you know, at this point, you come this far, a day—two—little issues, two days tops.

*Oldest enters.*

**OLDEST**   She's waiting in the car.

**FATHER**   My wife's waiting in the car. We've got a wedding. Two accountants. To each other. A food processor. It was on the registry. It's a list you, uh, get and, uh, you pick something they want—and you want to get 'em—so everybody's happy. Yes, it saves time and grief. Well, someday maybe you'll have a wedding. (*beat*) Look, it's no problem, it's just we gotta make for sure. We won't put you out past Thursday. Well, I'm glad too. Okay, talk to you. Righto. (*hangs up phone*) What's she doing in the goddam car?

**OLDEST** She says it's peaceful.

*Father and Oldest go outside. The phone rings again. Youngest comes downstairs wearing a bathrobe. She picks up the phone. It is 1:15 P.M.*

**YOUNGEST** His girlfriend waited in the lounge . . . ? You're a manager too! When did they make a rule? A rule about managers' girlfriends in the lounge? I just sat there and read *People*. I didn't vandalize a wall . . . Why would I want to Magic Marker—I don't get that, I don't. Fine. Fine. Good. (*sneezes*) Mold, I told you mold! Gone. A wedding. Yes. (*beat*) I can just show up, they're holding my classes. My, uh, ticket, I can move around the return date and school— they're holding—yeah. I'm preregistered, what's the problem? The airline gave me a free ticket to anywhere since the aborted you-know-what. (*beat*) Well, vote for who you want, but I never trusted his look. (*beat*) No, I don't see the point if I have to wait in the hallway frankly, no. Then—yes. For once you can. They'll be asleep. At two-thirty they'll be asleep! I miss it. My door locks. (*beat*) Okay, but I don't want to hear she's allowed in the lounge and I'm not. I don't want to hear that through people. I don't want to hear about any more people talking about me because there is simply no need!

*She hangs up and lies down on the couch. It is 5:00 A.M. Sunday, the next morning. Oldest enters from outside. She wakes up.*

**YOUNGEST** You're not him.

**OLDEST**   Shh, I'm not drunk. I don't have a key and the door's locked so I crawled through the trapdoor!

**YOUNGEST**   You're not him and it's—

**OLDEST**   The trapdoor! In the basement, when we had the haunted house?

**YOUNGEST**   It's five . . . five?

**OLDEST**   You'll never guess who I saw! That kid from your year. That dweeb in a tux.

**YOUNGEST**   (*looking at the alarm clock*)   Does that say five?

**OLDEST**   This bar, this place downtown.

**YOUNGEST**   It's five.

**OLDEST**   The new high-speed line goes downtown! And there you are . . . downtown! And there are these bars and happy downtown people all happy to be downtown and out of the suburbs. And they say come, come, come into our bars.

**YOUNGEST**   And none of them are women.

**OLDEST**   Some of them, but very few. And you'll never guess who I saw!

**YOUNGEST**   I didn't vandalize the fucking wall.

**OLDEST**   And we had drinks! (*beat*) We skipped something . . .

**YOUNGEST**   Where he works there was this incident and I am the prime suspect, or something.

**OLDEST**   Where?

**YOUNGEST**   At where he's a systems reengineerer.

**OLDEST**   Who?

**YOUNGEST**  I told you.

**OLDEST**  The boy you can transfer?

**YOUNGEST**  They can transfer him anywhere after six months, they can transfer me anywhere already. We can transfer all over the country when we want to and she stared at me and I wouldn't wait in the lounge and now the little games, the little games.

**OLDEST**  (*beat*)  You don't remember the haunted house?

**YOUNGEST**  And I bet she's the wall culprit and I bear the brunt of the new girlfriend rule.

**OLDEST**  I was a head on a platter, ketchup for blood?

**YOUNGEST**  He's scared.

**OLDEST**  We're skipping all over and it's really—

**YOUNGEST**  He's scared.

**OLDEST**  Oh. That. (*beat*) The thing about when you're drunk is that you've got to be simple and you are so thankful for that. (*beat*) We had drinks, c'mon!? (*beat*) You should go back to school.

**YOUNGEST**  You don't even think so.

**OLDEST**  Do as I say, do as I say! There's a window of something—when God shuts a door he opens another one—oh forget it. What's God care about ventilation?

**YOUNGEST**  You're so blasted.

**OLDEST**  C'mon, guess! Drinks. One after the other—they kept coming. Guess.

**YOUNGEST**  You shouldn't drink.

**OLDEST**  You won't, I swear. They kept coming, some in bottles, some in glasses. With a logo with a hat. A little pirate hat on a big mug. Inside the beer, like this— (*demonstrates sloshing*) The sea! (*beat*) Jonathan fucking hates the beach, which bugs me! (*beat*) Guess, guess. Come, come, come into the bar! Who said that?

**YOUNGEST**  I don't know.

**OLDEST**  I don't know.

**YOUNGEST**  You're saying guess!

**OLDEST**  You know him! Your year, you went out with his someone. He made that ashtray? That won over yours? You cried, you cried! We made a special ashtray award here, you hated it—he was wearing a tux?

**YOUNGEST**  You're kidding.

**OLDEST**  Who wears a tux? He said at the opera they wear tuxes and that's where he was but where was his program? And are there bars at the opera 'cause this guy was blasted!

**YOUNGEST**  Tommy Breznian.

**OLDEST** (*beat*)  The bar was Long John Silver's so it was his little pirate hat! (*beat*) No one's kissed me in such a long time. And he's going to do my taxes! I love the high-speed line! You pass the same things you do in a car but faster. The same route but you're higher up, like it's like model trains 'cause you're a giant, you're a fast giant and all the little houses aren't real, like this ride of transportation you're on! And you think it'll keep going 'cause there aren't any stops . . . but then it does and you get off and something about your body's still going even though you're still? You're on the platform and something inside keeps going— stop. Oh stop oh stop.

**YOUNGEST** (*beat*)   How were your last tests?

**OLDEST** (*he puts his head in her lap*)   Stop for a while.

**YOUNGEST**   The numbers?

**OLDEST**   In one place. (*beat*) Tests, tests, what are tests? What do numbers mean? (*beat*) There's a new treatment. It works for some people. I can go on it with this new insurance. (*beat*) Brick says to Maggie, "I'm waiting for the click." (*smiles*) Haha! You're listening!

**YOUNGEST**   Jonathan likes the beach, he's just—too much sun's not supposed to be good for you, right?

**OLDEST** (*looking around at the room*)   How many times have we seen this room almost asleep?

**YOUNGEST**   He wants you there.

**OLDEST** (*beat*)   After all this time, I know where everything is too.

**YOUNGEST** (*beat*)   You didn't come home to talk to me . . .

**OLDEST**   There's something behind your ear.

*He produces a quarter from her hair. The phone rings and Youngest picks it up fast.*

**YOUNGEST**   Don't call this late! (*beat*) Who is this? They're asleep upstairs . . . ? Okay. (*writes something down*) Yes, sir. Thank you. (*hangs up*) They're not upstairs.

**OLDEST**   What?

**YOUNGEST**   We've got to go to a hospital. A hospital that's far away.

*They get up and leave the house. They return leading Mother and Father, who both wear neck braces. They sit their parents on the couch, crouching beside them. It is 10:00 A.M.*

**MOTHER**  It was nobody's fault. And it's true, your whole life passes in front of your eyes, like a movie. Except I was watching this movie and it wasn't about me. When we were at the hospital later and I thought about it I thought, yeah, I guess that was about me. But when it was happening I thought: this movie is somebody's life, but whose?

**FATHER**  It was my fault, I was driving.

**MOTHER**  They're working on the road and all the signs are . . . convoluted.

**FATHER**  One sign was way high up, I don't know how you're supposed to see that.

**OLDEST**  Right, when Jonathan and I go to the beach—?

**FATHER**  Still and all I shoulda seen it.

**OLDEST**  We rent a car and we go to this beach, way far out and they're always working on the roads and the signs! You know, forget it!

**FATHER**  (*beat*)  You know, the buyer's a bachelor.

**MOTHER**  He knows that.

**OLDEST**  We don't go that often 'cause Jonathan burns easily.

**MOTHER**  (*to Father*)  What does that mean, what?

**FATHER**  What?

**YOUNGEST**  He doesn't mean—

**MOTHER**  He's single, not everyone's—

**FATHER**  He's single.

**YOUNGEST**  Don't try and turn.

**MOTHER**  Some people are just single.

**FATHER**   And some people are just married!

**YOUNGEST**   I thought you were asleep upstairs when they called.

**FATHER**   We were doped up but we weren't asleep.

**YOUNGEST**   In a minute we'll go through pills, dosages.

**MOTHER**   I'm not taking any more pills, I will not have my daughter sorting out pills. (*beat*) We are not "doped up." Please.

**OLDEST** (*beat*)   How was the wedding?

**MOTHER**   The wedding never happened! They could never find the groom!

**OLDEST**   What?

**YOUNGEST** (*to Oldest*)   Tell you later.

**MOTHER**   That's the first time that's happened.

**OLDEST**   My God!

**YOUNGEST** (*to Oldest*)   Tell you later, won't believe it.

**MOTHER**   We were all standing there like dummies waiting for this groom—

**FATHER**   And then they announced this thing—

**MOTHER**   —and but everybody stayed like it was some big party!

**FATHER**   Apparently they had some sense of—

**MOTHER**   The bride had a suspicion and she just laughed and everybody stayed. Which is weird. But we stayed too.

**FATHER**   And drank.

**MOTHER** We did not have that much! And by the time we were driving—

**FATHER** Whoa, by the time we were driving—pff.

**MOTHER** Well, we found ourselves with a few hours we thought we didn't have. Which doesn't happen often. So we drove. And one of us had the bright idea—

**FATHER** It was me.

**MOTHER** One of us, we're not sure, had this idea to go to the diner where we first met. (*she raises her hand*) Ow.

**OLDEST** Don't, just don't gesture.

**FATHER** This diner doesn't exist.

**MOTHER** It's long gone. We find this out—(*she gestures again*) ow.

**YOUNGEST** Don't!

**MOTHER** A state trooper gives me this information when I'm on my back on a stretcher. But at the time—

**FATHER** I thought I saw it last year.

**MOTHER** We were going from memory, at the time.

**FATHER** All the way at the end of the Blue Route.

**MOTHER** But thirty years!

**FATHER** Right before I-95.

**MOTHER** Still, we kept driving. Trying to remember, going farther away, driving, driving. Which was very nice.

**FATHER** You get off all the way at the end of the Blue Route and it shoulda been right there.

**MOTHER**  All those big new roads.

**FATHER**  (*beat*)  Ow.

**YOUNGEST**  Will you stop, both of you?

**MOTHER**  We forgot all about the groom . . . driving . . . the house . . . driving . . . our children. We were children.

**YOUNGEST**  You're not children.

**FATHER**  Boy, the Blue Route, you can get on that thing and just go! You can get to anywhere from there in half the time it used to take!

**MOTHER**  We just had this time that fell from the sky after a wedding that never happened.

*The phone rings.*

**YOUNGEST**  We are the children—(*to* oldest, *re: phone*) Get that.

**FATHER**  How could I miss that sign?

**OLDEST**  (*answering phone*)  Hello? Ohmygod—ohmygod, but Claudio's there though?

**FATHER**  You know, once last year they couldn't find the groom.

**OLDEST**  (*on phone*)  Uh, there's been an accident.

**YOUNGEST**  Don't say that!

**MOTHER**  But that one turned up finally.

**OLDEST**  (*on phone*)  No, my parents.

**FATHER**  He turned up after a while.

**OLDEST**  (*on phone*)  This morning, a car.

**FATHER**  This one yesterday never turned up. It was outside, everyone was sunburned.

144

**MOTHER**  Sometimes they're late and you think—uh-oh—but they usually—

**OLDEST** (*on phone*)  Look, I know—

**MOTHER**  Except for in movies.

**OLDEST** (*on phone*)  In the storeroom—what?

**FATHER**  In movies they never show up. That's what always happens. One or the other, they never show up.

**YOUNGEST**  I should do something—

**MOTHER**  And it was like a movie passing before your eyes but by the wrong studio, I kept thinking. You think: mainstream, mainstream, big stars. Paramount Pictures! But it looked European. I didn't recognize any of the stars.

**YOUNGEST**  I should be doing something!

**OLDEST** (*on phone*)  What?

**FATHER**  Maybe it's early Alzheimer's.

**MOTHER**  Oh, for God's sake—

**FATHER** (*to Mother*)  Can you turn this way?

**MOTHER**  No, I can't turn.

**YOUNGEST**  You can't turn that way?

**FATHER**  Who's he on with?

**OLDEST** (*on phone*)  Okay, look, listen . . .

**YOUNGEST**  Ohmygod, I need the phone!

**OLDEST** (*on phone*)  Have Claudio call me.

**YOUNGEST**  I didn't call work!

OLDEST (*on phone*)   You're three thousand miles away!

YOUNGEST   They gave me tomorrow off if I could work today!

MOTHER   They'll understand.

YOUNGEST   Everyone's off!

OLDEST (*on phone*)   Under the stairs, but—

FATHER   It's a holiday weekend—

OLDEST (*on phone*)   Exactly, but—

FATHER   Accidents are ten times likelier—

YOUNGEST   Don't say "accident"!

FATHER   That's what we had!

MOTHER   You know, your father could've built that plane.

FATHER   Oh, for God's sake.

MOTHER   No, why not?

YOUNGEST   Everyone's off!

FATHER   We don't make those planes!

OLDEST (*on phone*)   Tell him it's clearly marked, it's "Kringle Candle."

YOUNGEST (*to Oldest*)   C'mon, c'mon!

OLDEST (*on phone*)   Kringle—as in Kris with a K—Candle?

FATHER   You know, this groom was a Democrat.

MOTHER (*tilting head up*)   Can you do this?

FATHER (*turning head*)   No, I can do side-side.

**YOUNGEST**   Can you do side-side . . . ?

**MOTHER**   (*tries, fails*)   I'll get there.

**OLDEST**   (*on phone*)   I don't care what Claudio says—I can't possibly be responsible for any melting.

**YOUNGEST**   Oh, God, I don't believe this . . . there were things on your mind—

**FATHER**   There was nothing on our minds!

**YOUNGEST**   You weren't watching signs—

**FATHER**   I was watching the road!

**YOUNGEST**   (*to Oldest*)   Give me the phone!

**MOTHER**   (*to Youngest*)   They'll have to understand things happen.

**OLDEST**   (*on phone*)   I have to stay!

**MOTHER**   They're people, after all!

**YOUNGEST**   The phone, the phone—! (*opening a bottle of pills*) This is all because of me! It's all my fault—!

**MOTHER**   Things're unforeseeable—

**YOUNGEST**   You should kick me out!

**MOTHER**   My daughter will not give me pills!

**OLDEST**   (*to his parents*)   Don't move your heads!

**FATHER**   We can't help it, they're attached!

*Youngest gets pills opened and Mother knocks them out of her hands.*
*They fly everywhere.*


*End of Act One.*

# ACT TWO

*It is 7:00 P.M., Sunday evening. Boxes are now everywhere. Father, still in neck brace, picks up the newspaper. Youngest stands near the door, dressed to go out.*

**YOUNGEST**  He's got tonight off.

**FATHER**  Enjoy yourself.

**YOUNGEST**  It's okay?

**FATHER**  Your brother's here.

**YOUNGEST**  How long do you keep that on?

**FATHER**  It's just a precautionary thing, in case something I didn't feel then I all of a sudden feel now. There's this thing that happens when something might, uh, kick in. She's gotta keep hers on for two weeks, so I'm keeping mine on for her too. So she doesn't look stupid all by herself.

**YOUNGEST**  You look like twins.

**FATHER**  (*smiles*)  Enjoy yourself. (*he scratches his neck*)

**YOUNGEST**  It's itchy?

**FATHER**  In through here.

**YOUNGEST**  (*scratches the back of Father's head*)  I hope you know. I hope you know—

**FATHER**  Nah, nuh.

**YOUNGEST**  (*beat*)  We're going in for dinner. We split it, dutch. (*beat*) School? My questions? I'm not being difficult for difficulty's sake. I still have my plane ticket. I keep it in my purse.

148

**FATHER**   You see the tab back there?

**YOUNGEST**   This?

**FATHER**   Pull it back.

**YOUNGEST**   Here? This?

**FATHER**   Careful, yeah.

**YOUNGEST** (*she opens his neck brace and massages his neck*)   You know, I'm not just—

**FATHER**   All of you like to talk. You ever read a paper? I never see a paper.

**YOUNGEST** (*beat*)   You'd like him.

**FATHER**   I like people.

**YOUNGEST**   He consolidates systems.

**FATHER**   Bring him 'round.

**YOUNGEST**   That's when you've got all these divergent systems from over the years and you want to get streamlined.

**FATHER**   Bring him 'round.

**YOUNGEST**   You don't bite.

**FATHER**   Your mother bites. She's got big teeth. (*taps his teeth*) I just bark.

**YOUNGEST**   What if you had to pay per tooth size?

**FATHER**   Aw, forget it.

**YOUNGEST**   The other night we were talking about him maybe getting a transfer near to school so for my last year— if I decided to go back—he could be nearby.

**FATHER**  Huh.

**YOUNGEST**  They need what he does everywhere. It doesn't sound like it but they do.

**FATHER**  Huh.

**YOUNGEST**  But he was dead against the whole idea because if you're a manager, which he is, you can't send this signal to your company all the time like you're ready to leave all the time until you maintain a position of authority for a sufficient period of time and then you can. He's not in a place to send that signal. He's not there yet.

**FATHER**  (*beat*)  There'll be other buyers.

**YOUNGEST**  If I brought him around? Maybe for dinner?

**FATHER**  I'd make my famous mashed potatoes.

**YOUNGEST**  That's all guys make, mashed potatoes, like it's some big deal!

**FATHER**  Fine, I won't.

**YOUNGEST**  He knows you. When he was little, fourteen, something, you yelled at him about his bike on the lawn.

**FATHER**  He knows me?

**YOUNGEST**  He was delivering circulars and he rode his bike on the grass and you gave it to him.

**FATHER**  I wouldn't.

**YOUNGEST**  He said a bunch of times, yes.

**FATHER**  A kid with a bike?

**YOUNGEST**  (*beat*)  You don't—?

**FATHER**  I never yelled at the paperboys.

**YOUNGEST**   That doesn't sound familiar?

**FATHER**   The Catholic charities—

**YOUNGEST**   You terrorized him for like two years.

**FATHER**   Jehovah's Witness, never yelled.

**YOUNGEST**   Two years to a teenager!

**FATHER**   I terrorize no one—Salvation Army—

**YOUNGEST**   You do—everyone—you do!

**FATHER**   That was years ago! I'm sure he's all grown up and hairy now.

**YOUNGEST**   (*sneezes*)   Ucchh! I'm taking this huge antihistamine!

**FATHER**   You're twenty-two. These things, paperboys, tears, the lawn when you kids—shouldn't mean anything anymore. You've got a job, dean's list, a car—these—these—life keeps—tears, bikes, boys, so on—it—goes in—and before you know—before you know—

**YOUNGEST**   They're making you retire.

**FATHER**   (*beat*)   They've been good to me. (*beat*) No one's said that yet. (*beat*) There've been inferences.

**YOUNGEST**   You're not old enough.

**FATHER**   I'll get another job. There're other jobs. Paperboy! And if I retire I get a package, a whole deal—pension, we can stretch it. That doesn't come along every . . . No one's said that! (*beat*) Your hair looks pretty, down like that.

**YOUNGEST**   I had it cut.

**FATHER**   One day at a time.

*His head wobbles; she catches it.*

**FATHER**   Whoa—! There you go! Phew. (*beat*) You're the baby, you've always been the baby. (*beat*) I like this house. I'm comfortable. We know the neighbors. And they wave. That doesn't happen all over. Neighbors waving. Just read the papers. Neighbors are up to all kindsa stuff. We could close off rooms. I don't mind a basement flood every summer. The lawn—who cares? The leaves—you rake! She wants to keep the place clean—for what? We're all paid off! If we stretch things—but she's got worries.

**YOUNGEST**   He looks good.

**FATHER**   It'll all come out fine.

**YOUNGEST** (*puts his brace back on*)   For now.

*A horn honks outside.*

**YOUNGEST** (*cont.*)   You'd like him. He's like you.

**FATHER**   Who's he voting for?

**MOTHER** (*calling from upstairs*)   Is she down there?

**FATHER** (*calling up*)   She's going out.

**MOTHER**   Can I see her please?

**YOUNGEST** (*to Father about going out*)   I don't have to.

**FATHER**   I'll tell him to wait. (*taps his teeth*) Get a load of her teeth when you're up there.

*Father opens front door and signals for Youngest's boyfriend to wait. Youngest goes upstairs. Father sits. Youngest runs back on and out front door. Mother comes downstairs wearing her neck brace, but now there's a scarf tied around it, secured by a broach. Father takes off his neck brace and does neck stretches throughout. It is 8:00 P.M.*

**MOTHER**   So if we lose this buyer, you're perfectly fine?

**FATHER**   We won't lose him.

**MOTHER**   If Tuesday comes and goes and we lose this buyer she said you said you're perfectly fine about that. You like waving to people? You like waving to people on the block or something?

**FATHER**   That was a conversation.

**MOTHER**   And we are now—you and I are now having— where is she? I want her down here—

**FATHER**   She's at dinner.

**MOTHER**   (*calling upstairs*)   Young lady!

**FATHER**   She's at dinner, she's not upstairs.

**MOTHER**   And if you retire early, that's fine? That's all fine? To you that's fine.

**FATHER**   We've been in an accident! Will you sit down.

**MOTHER**   I'm fine.

**FATHER**   Your back is all screwy, the doctor said—

**MOTHER**   I know what he said.

**FATHER**   And if you're jerking around, all over—

**MOTHER**   I am standing, that's what I'm doing, I'm too high to sit! I am just standing. (*beat*) What do you mean jerking around? I am walking. I want him down here.

**FATHER**   He's taking a nap.

**MOTHER**   I don't care. (*calling upstairs*) Come down!

**FATHER**   Let the boy sleep.

**MOTHER**   Great, fine, everyone's sleeping. I'm glad people can sleep when I'm up all night—and you know! You know.

**FATHER** (*beat*)   There's the picnic tomorrow. You coming? (*beat*) Just make the macaroni.

**MOTHER**   We'll see. (*beat*) You make the macaroni. What am I, some kind of macaroni machine?

**FATHER**   Oh my God.

**MOTHER**   You think I can go to a picnic and sit in a chair like, what, like your mother sitting in her chair? You think we have eight kids and they're gonna have eight kids and all those, what, sixty-four kids and grandkids are gonna come to this house and mow the lawn and paint it when it needs it and pay for little repairs? That doesn't happen anymore, mister, things fall apart around people. Families don't exist! 'Cause he's not getting married, you know.

**FATHER**   Okay. Okay, okay.

**MOTHER**   No one's getting married anytime soon.

*Oldest comes downstairs wiping the sleep from his eyes.*

**MOTHER** (*cont.*)   Your father said you were taking a nap but I don't care.

**OLDEST**   Thanks.

**MOTHER**   No I don't, what if I took a nap? What if I dropped everything in this house and said—"Hey, I'm going to take a nap! You people take care of everything!"

**OLDEST**   Well, you know, we wouldn't. We'd probably just leave and go to a movie.

**MOTHER** (*beat*)   Your father doesn't want to move.

**OLDEST**   Well, I didn't either but you were screaming.

**MOTHER**   (*beat*)   I don't think this was the first buyer. Maybe your father scared others off.

**FATHER**   She's always screaming.

**MOTHER**   Well, I need to be heard.

**OLDEST**   Through the floor?

**FATHER**   She was louder when you were young.

**OLDEST**   The both of your voices.

**FATHER**   Lost some lung power.

**MOTHER**   I need to be heard!

**FATHER**   Okay, okay.

**OLDEST**   The walls, the floor—

**FATHER**   Will you tell her—

**OLDEST**   You woke me.

**MOTHER**   You tell me something!

**FATHER**   Will you take a minute and tell your mother—

**OLDEST**   Your voices.

**MOTHER**   No, you tell me, I don't need to be told anything.

**FATHER**   When you said you wanted to move I said fine!

**MOTHER**   You said fine, oh, yeah.

**OLDEST**   The floor's thin.

**MOTHER**   You said fine to placate me. And then on about your business.

**FATHER**  Yes.

**MOTHER**  On about your business.

**FATHER**  I go to work! I get up and go to work, you don't think I work?

**MOTHER**  (*beat*)  No.

**FATHER**  (*beat*)  You don't think when I get up at five—

**OLDEST**  She gets up at five.

**MOTHER**  I think you talk to all your old school buddies.

**FATHER**  Aw, c'mon!

**MOTHER**  And call that work, yes, I think you go to lunch and talk to buddies! My boss doesn't take me to lunch! I don't have a boss who comes to the house when I get off work, brings over my buddies, and says—"C'mon! We're going out! It's on me!"

**OLDEST**  How do people talk this way?

**MOTHER**  I don't have that!

**FATHER**  This is the way she talks!

**OLDEST**  I'm almost thirty for fuck's sake! And I don't know how to talk! (*beat*) How to talk. I don't know, I have all these things to say, things I should be saying! But he's always saying—"Move in!" But—I'm still saying these *nothing* things, that aren't anything to do with what should now BE SAID! Things should now be said! But I'm still saying these all-around things! Things you've said—things I've heard asleep, upstairs. (*beat*) I borrowed a sweater. It smells like potpourri. (*beat*) That makes sense, my room, storage. I'm hardly ever home.

156

*The phone rings. Father picks it up.*

**FATHER**   Hey-ho! Hallarya! Yeah, Thursday. (*beat*) Well, tomorrow's the holiday. Oh, sure, uh-huh. Sure, uh-huh. Nah, we're here all day.

**MOTHER**   The picnic.

**FATHER**   We've got a picnic. Well—huh—yeah, yeah—you gotta do what you gotta do. Okay, okay, will do. Good talking. Righto. (*hangs up phone*) There's another house he likes. His girlfriend likes. He likes this one. Tomorrow they gotta know.

**OLDEST**   Can I—

**MOTHER**   What girlfriend?

**OLDEST**   Can I—

**FATHER**   She came by at an open house.

**MOTHER**   Without—

**FATHER**   He wants this one, he's the one buying it.

**MOTHER**   She walked through the house and didn't—what, judging? Liking another house better—judging us? Who is this girlfriend all of a sudden?

**FATHER**   She'll take this one, fine, okay, but she doesn't want to jeopardize losing the other house if we say sorry on Tuesday. Tomorrow, that's all. Tomorrow we tell him.

**MOTHER**   It's supposed to be a holiday tomorrow. (*beat*) What was all this bachelor business? (*beat*) Where is your sister having dinner? When did she go?

**OLDEST**   Can I.

*The phone rings and Father picks it up.*

**FATHER**  Eyah? (*hands phone to Oldest*)

**OLDEST**  Yeah? (*beat*) Under the Baby Jesus night-light. Under the Baby Jesus carton. For safekeeping. That's it, we're buying Claudio a beeper. Yes, look—purple. No— what? What? (*sighs*) Fuck you. (*hangs up*)

**MOTHER**  Don't keep saying that!

**OLDEST**  I'm fired!

**MOTHER**  Why does anybody have to say those words, I don't care!

**OLDEST**  Jonathan fired me.

**FATHER**  (*to Mother*)  They can't wait past tomorrow.

**MOTHER**  Why can't he wait? I waited. I waited months for somebody to—(*beat*) Where is she? Where is she—I want her down here—

**OLDEST**  She's at dinner!

**FATHER**  Downtown with the paperboy!

**MOTHER**  I've waited a lifetime out in the middle of nowhere with people I don't know—we don't know half these people on this block here and I've waited years!

**OLDEST**  What are you saying?

**MOTHER**  With dreams, expectations—but things come up! Things happen, life comes up and—

**OLDEST**  What are you saying?

**MOTHER**  Some people can afford things! Some people have leeway!

**OLDEST**  WHAT?!

**MOTHER**  WE WON'T HAVE MONEY IF YOU GET SICK! We won't have money—and I've seen it! People come back sick and that's it—that's your whole life waiting on someone in a room and I've waited—! We'll end up watching TV, with hot plates, rooms closed off. My father lived to ninety! In those pants. I hemmed his pants do you think she—? Your sister hemming pants? Your father out of work—the money for a hospital—the house falling down—and that's what happens! How do we live? How do we live! (*She runs upstairs.*)

**FATHER**  (*after a beat, calling upstairs*)  You're just excited! Everyone's excited.

**OLDEST**  (*beat*)  Can someone drive me to the train station?

*Father goes upstairs. Oldest sits and picks up phone. It is 9:00 p.m. Father comes downstairs with a small hand made book.*

**OLDEST**  I'm on hold. (*beat*) It's a holiday schedule. Tomorrow. Tonight we're into Sunday, Sunday evening—nothing. From this little tape they're running. They're running this little tape, the times, departing times, excursion rate—not—holiday fare, holiday—(*beat*) I'm still on hold. (*beat*) I'm waiting for a person, not a little voice.

**FATHER**  There's the bus.

**OLDEST**  Then that's, that's you driving me all the way to 12th and Arch, waiting there with homeless people, seats with spilled . . . candy corns. Five hours, with all the stops—once you're on. It's five hours of like absolutely no leg room. And the seats never work, the lean seats. (*demonstrates*) You're sitting straight up. On a bus on a bed of crushed candy corns.

**FATHER**  Stay the night, get up early.

**OLDEST** If I get up in my own bed tomorrow—it's just this thing. (*beat*) If I get up in my own bed then it's a whole day that's mine, my life, whatever—or if I get up early here and go it's like half the day is not my life, it's some, you know, visitor's life, it's some person visiting some couch.

**FATHER** That can't be comfortable.

**OLDEST** It's fine, it's a couch. No, it's fine. But it's that. (*beat*) It's just a couch in a house somewhere as opposed to a bed, my bed, my home, my clock—little digital one that makes this little beeping sound I know. This one, this clock, it's like, what? One of your old army clocks?

**FATHER** I don't worry about you!

**OLDEST** The sound it makes is huge. It's like being machine-gunned awake.

**FATHER** No I don't. (*beat*) Found your book, that book. That bible. (*shows it*) Here's the colon. That's cute.

**OLDEST** Huh.

**FATHER** It's all here, Noah you got—

**OLDEST** I don't—

**FATHER** Moses here with the tablets.

**OLDEST** Oh, you know—

**FATHER** Those're good tablets. For a kid with a pencil.

**OLDEST** Pastels. Chalk. (*beat*) Let's not bring out old things.

**FATHER** You got up through Jesus, Abraham, Isaac—up through—something—what's that?

**OLDEST** What? (*looks*) That's a cave. For Lazarus.

**FATHER**  That's a cave.

**OLDEST**  It's a . . . big hole in a mountain or something. I don't—

**FATHER**  And then it says here—

**OLDEST**  It's a mountain entrance.

**FATHER**  Stuff you wrote.

**OLDEST**  Maybe we should just go to the station.

**FATHER**  Five, six . . . ?

**OLDEST**  Go, see what's leaving?

**FATHER**  What's second grade? You're six, seven—?

**OLDEST**  There's got to be a train, some point, sometime.

**FATHER**  Second grade? Little mind, all this stuff. (*reads*) "Then God said to Jesus—get up! You're not dead anymore! I know you're pretending! There's a better place and you're gonna miss out!" Then there's something, some kiddy hieroglyphics.

**OLDEST** (*looking*)  I don't know.

**FATHER**  Something.

**OLDEST**  Something . . .

**FATHER** (*reading*)  "Come to my House—it's up high. It's more high up than"—and then you number things—"more high up than 1. Upstairs 2. The attic. 3. The birds and trees even."

**OLDEST** (*on phone*)  It's still this little voice.

**FATHER**  "But we got pizza up here." Pizza up here!

**OLDEST**   I read an article about this little voice person. She's some teacher in Idaho.

**FATHER**   Guess you liked pizza. "Signed"—and then another colon—"God." That's a whole little book.

**OLDEST**   The airlines pick up, right up. Last week, Thursday, Jonathan wanted me to fly out for the weekend, have Claudio open and I just called the airline no problem.

**FATHER**   I guess you were just big on colons.

**OLDEST**   *(beat)*   I can't just go wherever he is whenever he calls. You can't just drop everything when someone, I don't care who—

**FATHER**   We called.

**OLDEST**   *(beat)*   What I don't get is for big trips, hurling tons of a flying machine thirty thousand feet through the sky, it's no problem to get scheduling information. A hundred miles, a choo-choo train on a track, is suddenly now a problem. *(beat)* You can't just keep going wherever another person calls from. I've got my own place. It's a sublet, but . . . Well, it's not legal but, not yet. *(beat)* It's not my bed even really. It was pre . . . furnished.

**FATHER**   *(beat)*   What, boy?

**OLDEST**   *(beat)*   He keeps saying there's reason to hope—and I—want to tell him—it's hard to think so.

**MOTHER**   *(after a beat, calling from upstairs)*   Is he down there? *(beat)* Answer me, I can hear you both.

**FATHER**   *(calling up)*   If you can hear us both, why you asking? Huh?

**MOTHER**   *(beat)*   Can I see him?

**OLDEST** (*calling up*)   I'm on hold, I can't get off now or I lose my place.

**MOTHER** (*beat*)   What?

**OLDEST** (*with Father*)   I'm on hold, I can't hang up—

**FATHER** (*calling up*)   Why does everybody have to come up or down to wherever you are? YOU come down. (*beat*) Huh? (*holding up book*) She'd kill me if she knew I kept unpacking this. (*starts to go*) If she got sick, I'd . . . I wouldn't . . . we'd all find a way. (*beat*) That's good to know about . . . things.

*Father goes upstairs. Oldest falls asleep on couch with the phone in hand. Mother comes downstairs, without neck brace, and hangs up phone. She begins to unpack things from the many boxes and put them back in their place. After a moment, Youngest comes in from outside. It is midnight.*

**MOTHER**   We were going to drive him to the train station, but he fell asleep. (*Mother unpacks a deck of cards and magician's interlocking rings.*)

**YOUNGEST**   I'll drive him tomorrow.

**MOTHER**   There's the picnic, your cousins, in the afternoon.

**YOUNGEST**   Did you make the macaroni?

**MOTHER**   Did your father ask you to ask me that? (*beat*) Your aunts make enough. Their mother had a recipe. They like to keep making the same recipe for some reason.

**YOUNGEST**   It's just a side dish.

**MOTHER**   In your little talk did your father ask you to ask me about macaroni?

**YOUNGEST**   There's six tons of the same side dish.

**MOTHER**  Well, it's the same casserole every year and I'm not going.

**YOUNGEST**  You should be asleep.

**MOTHER**  Your father's snoring.

**YOUNGEST**  It's late and your neck.

**MOTHER**  He sleeps like a baby, snoring. You kept me up. You were loud when you were hungry. But you didn't want my breast, you liked the bottle. You always made a little face. (*she makes the face*) You go tomorrow, go with your father. Bring your friend. Bring potato salad, see how that goes over. (*beat*) What will we do if they make him retire? He's got no hobbies. He's too young to be an old person.

**YOUNGEST**  He'll do something.

**MOTHER**  We'd like to enjoy life. (*she unpacks a magician's top hat*) Your brother, from job to job.

**YOUNGEST**  He likes that.

**MOTHER**  Magicians don't have insurance. (*beat*) Your sister. My baby. I can't go through that again.

**YOUNGEST** (*beat*)  Mother?

**MOTHER**  No, fine, go to the picnic, I'm glad everyone can go to picnics.

**YOUNGEST**  Mom? (*beat*) He loves me.

**MOTHER** (*beat*)  That's very nice. That's very nice and I'm sure you're both, you've both been—both—I'm not judging. I'm not proud of that. You love him, you're safe, I'll turn an ear. Your father was the only one. (*beat*) We got a call. We're on a different . . . timetable. And if there's still any chance—school? A little chance?

**YOUNGEST**  He loves me.

**MOTHER**  (*beat*)  At least we won't be lonely. Some people are lonely.

**YOUNGEST**  We've been talking—for months now—and we talked about, you know, all kinds of things, options—there's lots. And we eventually came 'round to the thought we had—well he had it first and then I had it but I said it first and he was blown away because he'd been thinking it and there I was just blurting it out and that was we'd move in together. As a trial thing. As something we'd try. And there's always college here next semester and then if things go sort of maybe not so bad like we're thinking we'd . . . get married a year from next Easter. Whenever that falls. I mean he's really doing well here. All these people want new systems.

**MOTHER**  We haven't met this person.

**YOUNGEST**  Well, Daddy knows him.

**MOTHER**  Your father knows this person?

**YOUNGEST**  For years, yeah.

**MOTHER**  Why wouldn't he say that? Why wouldn't he tell me that?

**YOUNGEST**  He wants me to move in soon. If I say yes, I'd move out. You could say yes to the buyer.

**MOTHER**  (*beat*)  Well, that's silly. (*beat*) Not your age.

**YOUNGEST**  Soon, you know—if I tell him yes.

**MOTHER**   That's just silly, that's an answer? That's an answer to your problem?

**YOUNGEST**   I won't do it if you say no.

**MOTHER**   You see? (*beat*) You see?

**YOUNGEST**   No——? Tell me. (*beat*) Let's go shopping tomorrow. We'll get you new glasses. Some pretty frames? That could bring out your eyes? I wish I had your eyes.

*Father comes downstairs in his pajamas, paging through Oldest's bible.*

**FATHER**   . . . Everyone's up, that's a sign of something . . .

*Oldest wakes on couch.*

**OLDEST**   What?

**YOUNGEST**   Mother?

**FATHER**   . . . everyone's up . . .

**YOUNGEST**   Mommy?

**OLDEST** (*sees his Father with the bible*)   Why do you keep—

**FATHER**   Such a little mind.

**OLDEST**   —unpacking that? Please.

**FATHER**   Imagine a kid thinking so much about heaven.

*Oldest takes the bible from his Father and is about to tear it.*

**FATHER** (*cont.*)   Don't—! (*grabbing the bible from Oldest*) That's not yours, that's mine! You didn't keep that, that's ours, we kept it! Do you know what she's thrown out? Everything! She kept that. She kept that. What will I have to look at with all this free time I'm looking at?

**OLDEST** (*beat*)  No one think about heaven anymore. Please? I'm tired of thinking about . . .

**YOUNGEST** (*beat*)  Why is everybody looking at me? How can you be looked at?! What did I do? I didn't fuck up—

**MOTHER**  Don't say that.

**YOUNGEST**  I didn't fuck up, I didn't get sick—

**MOTHER**  DON'T SAY THAT!

**YOUNGEST**  I just took the wrong plane! I didn't get pregnant like half of everybody. All I did was get straight A's and get on THE WRONG FUCKING PLANE! (*taking her plane ticket from her purse and handing it to Oldest*) Take this. And the receipt and the boarding pass—and go!

**MOTHER**  What are you giving him?

**YOUNGEST**  Go!

*Youngest runs out of the house. Mother follows to door.*

**MOTHER**  WHERE ARE YOU GOING?

**FATHER** (*whispering*)  The neighbors!

**MOTHER**  I don't care. They never knew me. This was never a home. (*calling outside*) THEY NEVER KNEW THIS WAS NEVER A HOME!

*Father pulls Mother away from the door, and when she's inside he waves to a neighbor outside.*

**OLDEST** (*he looks at the plane ticket in his hands, then picks up the phone and dials*) Hey, it's me. Can I—? What's . . . behind your ear? (*beat*) That won't get your much. (*beat*) I want to come home. I want to . . . say things. Okay. (*stops before hanging up*) The thing is—where are you?

167

*Father and Mother go upstairs. Oldest packs his overnight bag. It is
9:00 A.M. Monday, the next morning. It is raining outside. Mother
comes downstairs, dressed for the picnic.*

**MOTHER**   You have everything?

**OLDEST**   I just brought the bag.

**MOTHER**   Did you look in the fridge? I can wrap up things.

**OLDEST**   Nah, I always forget and then I find all this food
days later in my bag.

**MOTHER**   Just unpack first thing. Set down your bag, unpack!
(*smiles*) Why do I know everything?

**OLDEST**   She's not back?

**MOTHER**   It won't be the first night. (*beat*) And do you have
to go in rain? Can you change the flight?

**OLDEST**   They fly in rain.

**MOTHER**   Well, the picnic's canceled, so—(*she looks outside*)
Oh, he's not ready yet.

**OLDEST**   He's sorting through the recycling.

**MOTHER**   They make you separate the colored glass.

**OLDEST**   He's been out there all morning.

**MOTHER**   He likes the garbage. (*beat*) The Breznian boy
showed up. Just a case of the willies, I guess. So it's a good
thing your father didn't return the food processor. They're
rescheduling for a few months down the line.

**OLDEST**   You'll have another buyer and be packed and out of
here!

MOTHER  Don't get my hopes up! (*beat*) Maybe. Hopefully. Maybe it's our ad. (*picking up the real estate section of the newspaper*) Look at this one. (*reads*) "One-family brick, minutes from DuPont Gardens." Well. Fancy. What are we near? We must be near something that makes us seem—to people who don't know us—special. (*beat*) Well—L.A.! The coast!

OLDEST  Well, you know.

MOTHER  Hollywood!

OLDEST  It's outside of Hollywood. But it's all right there, you know.

MOTHER  Celebrities.

OLDEST  And Jonathan's place is amazing. It's completely clay. And it's in the Canyons.

MOTHER  A clay house in the Canyons.

OLDEST  Yeah.

MOTHER  Jonathan with the hair.

OLDEST  He cut it. When you met him—

MOTHER  Do people live in clay houses?

OLDEST  Uh . . . like an adobe.

MOTHER  Oh, sure.

OLDEST  There's plumbing. I mean, it's designed like an adobe but there's central air and everything. From what he's told me. (*looks outside*) Better check for the ticket now.

MOTHER  That's all okay, exchanging—?

OLDEST  There was a little trouble with the airline when I called.

169

**MOTHER**  Well, it's a free ticket and they don't want just anybody—

**OLDEST**  They said it could transfer to family—

**MOTHER**  You know, any stranger—

**OLDEST**  They make exceptions for family.

**MOTHER**  They should, they really should. (*beat*) Before? Last night? That business . . . ? (*beat*) We're so proud of you. We're so proud.

**OLDEST**  Mom.

**MOTHER**  Enid calls all the time and asks, what's he doing? And I say all these things. We don't do much, we sit and hear about things. The TV, sometimes, not much. You see things, in the paper, friends tell us about things secondhand. You can spend a whole life just hearing about real life somewhere else. But you do things. I tell Enid. Imagine. He finds quarters! He makes things happen for children! All that, whatever he wants, he goes places, wherever. No worries. He should have worries. We're so proud. Your father. (*beat*) When people are over he gives them the update. I get jealous hearing about it. Then I remember, I know him. I more than know you. (*beat*) I wanted a girl. I'm not bad. You don't mind me?

**OLDEST**  Mom.

**MOTHER**  Before? Yesterday? All that . . .

**OLDEST**  Nothing.

**MOTHER**  I get excited.

**OLDEST**  Don't—forget it.

**MOTHER** When I do my exercises I calm down. *Sweating to the Oldies.* A video your sister got me. Corny. But it helps.

**OLDEST** You should take baths.

**MOTHER** I'm susceptible to infections, the water.

**OLDEST** From *baths*?

**MOTHER** We traced it to the bath.

**OLDEST** There's got to be something—I take a bath and, you know, all that water surrounding—the world!

**MOTHER** (*beat*) You look rested.

**OLDEST** All I do is sleep when I visit.

**MOTHER** You got some rest. We could all use rest.

**OLDEST** It's the age we live in.

**MOTHER** (*smiles*) No discounts then?

**OLDEST** (*smiles*) I got canned!

**MOTHER** I wish they'd can me.

**OLDEST** I left some money for the phone calls.

**MOTHER** No! Where? Absolutely not! Where?

*Mother goes off to the kitchen. After a moment, Youngest comes in from outside.*

**YOUNGEST** When you're with him, are you scared?

**OLDEST** No.

**YOUNGEST** Me either. (*she goes to the phone and makes a call*) It's me. Walking all night. Thinking. Thinking "Okay." Yes, I'm saying okay. Yes, okay means yes. Yes! Okay. (*about to hang up*) Hey—can we—can we take a trip soon? Okay.

*Mother comes in holding cash. Youngest is hanging up phone.*

**YOUNGEST**  Next month there's an apartment opening in his building. I said okay.

*Father comes in from outside.*

**MOTHER** (*to Father*)  Next month there's an apartment opening in his building. She said okay.

**FATHER**  Huh. (*beat*) Well, we should call the buyer.

**MOTHER**  Yes.

*Everyone looks at the house for a moment.*

**FATHER** (*to Oldest*)  You ready?

**OLDEST**  Yeah.

**FATHER**  Did you get food?

**MOTHER**  He doesn't want to carry it.

**FATHER**  Doesn't want to carry it?

**MOTHER**  He leaves it in his bag, I don't know.

**YOUNGEST** (*to Oldest*)  Call.

*Youngest holds her brother.*

**FATHER** (*beat*)  Okay, okay, we gotta roll here!

**MOTHER**  Okay, and—

**OLDEST**  We'll see about the holidays.

**MOTHER**  Okay, just check.

**FATHER** (*beat*)  Okay, we're rolling!

**OLDEST**  It all depends on where I am.

**MOTHER**  Okay, you just—(*cries*)

**OLDEST**  Don't.

**MOTHER**  Too much. (*wipes eyes*) You just have a good flight. Okay. Too much at once . . .

**FATHER**  C'mon, we're gonna stop by recycling, kill two birds.

**MOTHER**  You call!

**OLDEST**  I'll call!

**MOTHER**  (*she stops her son*)  Soon there will be good people in office, high and low, and things will change. People won't worry, jobs, you'll see, not so up and down. Things are happening, all the time—discoveries. Big ones. That could help us . . . *live!* I've lived some years and you'll see— everything—could change!

*Oldest and Father leave the house. Mother and Youngest stand in the open door.*

**MOTHER**  Well. (*beat*) He looks good.

**YOUNGEST**  You wanna still go shopping? Lenscrafters is open, I passed it. New frames?

**MOTHER**  (*beat*)  Tinted ones. A little more blue.

*Mother waves to the car pulling away outside.*


*Lights fade. End of Play.*

# THE BEGINNING
# OF AUGUST

For our father who art in heaven

Oh! Blessed rage for order, pale Ramon,

The maker's rage to order the words of the sea,

Words of the fragrant portals, dimly-starred,

And ourselves and of our origins,

In ghostlier demarcations, keener sounds.

—Wallace Stevens,
*The Idea of Order at Key West*

*The Beginning of August* was produced by Atlantic Theater Company (Neil Pepe, Artistic Director; Hillary Hinckle, Managing Director) in New York City on October 12, 2000. The play was directed by Neil Pepe. The scenery was designed by Scott Pask; the costumes by Ilona Somogyi; the lighting by Chris Akerlind; the music by Dave Carbonara; and the sound by Janet Kalas. The Stage manager was Jennifer Marik. The cast was:

| | |
|---|---|
| JACKIE | Garret Dillahunt |
| BEN | Jason Ritter |
| JOYCE | Mary Steenburgen |
| TED | Ray Anthony Thomas |
| PAM | Mary McCann |

*The Beginning of August* was originaly produced by South Coast Repertory (David Emmes, Producing Artisitc Director; Martin Benson, Artistic Director) on April 25 through May 28, 2000. The play was directed by Neil Pepe. The scenery was designed by Scott Pask; the costumes by Shigeru Yaji; the lighting by Chris Akerlind; the music and sound were by B. C. Keller. The dramaturg was Jennifer Kiger; the production manager was Jeff Gifford; the stage manager was Randall K. Lum; and the production assistant was Karen Barnett. The cast was as follows:

| | |
|---|---|
| JACKIE | Geoffrey Nauffts |
| BEN | Todd Lowe |
| JOYCE | Barbara Tarbuck |
| TED | Jeff Allin |
| PAM | Mary McCann |

# ACT ONE

*Morning. The sound of a lawn mower in the near distance. The back corner of a suburban house is seen: a door leading to the backyard, and a second floor window above it. Adjacent to the house, a blond wood fence runs the length of the lawn, which is very green. Against the fence is a bird feeder that resembles a small house. And, lining the edge of a stone path that cuts to the middle of the yard, there are electric lawn lanterns.*

*JACKIE, a man in his early thirties, is standing in the center of the lawn, looking down the drive. After a moment he opens a lawn chair leaning against the fence and places it in the center of the lawn. He looks down the drive again. He then returns to the fence where he finds a multicolored sun umbrella, which he fits into the back of the lawn chair. He looks down the drive again. He then goes into the house and returns with a portable bassinet. In it sleeps his infant daughter. He places the bassinet next to the lawn chair, in the shade of an unseen tree. Once again, he looks down the drive. He then goes to take the baby from the bassinet. He seems unable to. He is reaching out to the child one more time when BEN comes into the yard from the house, wiping paint from his hands. The sound of the lawn mower fades. Ben watches Jackie for a moment before Jackie realizes he's there.*

**BEN**    Everything's back where I found it.

**JACKIE**    Thank you.

**BEN**    So, if that's all you need?

**JACKIE**    For now. There's the whole hallway to do, of course. The corners, the trim, the molding around the edges around the wall. I'll call when we're up to it.

**BEN**    I don't mind going ahead.

**JACKIE**  Money's tight now.

**BEN**  Since I've started. The drop cloths are there.

**JACKIE**  We'll pay as we go. I'll pay as I go. Thank you, though.

**BEN**  It's not like I'm doing anything. The end of July there's nothing going on. I just sit home jerking off.

**JACKIE**  (*beat*)  We'll call. I'll call.

**BEN**  I'm gonna need to come and go today. Pick up my things.

**JACKIE**  But someone will be here, you should know. To sit for the baby. A woman will be here.

**BEN**  And I should interact with her?

**JACKIE**  I mention it so that you won't be alarmed when you see her.

**BEN**  What, is she ugly?

**JACKIE**  I was thinking you wouldn't expect to see her. She's not ugly. She's not anything. She's just an average lady with . . . sunglasses. So she's a stranger to you and she'll be around and there's no cause for alarm.

**BEN**  And Pam?

**JACKIE**  Nothing yet. That's why the woman's coming. I figured I should go ahead and get someone for during the day. With Pam gone. (*He looks at his child.*) A motherless child. There's a Negro spiritual that has that lyric.

**BEN**  I don't think people use that word anymore. (*Jackie takes out his checkbook.*) You know, I've been a baby-sitter, too. I can sit for kids.

180

**JACKIE**   No, no.

**BEN**   I can. I can sit.

**JACKIE**   How much did we say?

**BEN**   I've sat lots and lots.

**JACKIE**   Let's keep this professional.

**BEN**   You hired some lady.

**JACKIE**   She's my father's wife.

**BEN**   A father's wife is not professional.

*Jackie writes Ben's paycheck.*

**JACKIE**   I think we said this for the week.

**BEN**   I can be more professional than a father's wife. I'd do it for Pam.

*Jackie hands Ben his paycheck.*

**JACKIE**   Here's a tip. It should be bigger.

**BEN**   Pam gave me little breaks. Lemonade at the end of the day. Sometimes with a shot of something in it. I was all "whoa," pretending I didn't want it. Who wouldn't want it?

**JACKIE**   You know, that business about "jerking off" isn't appropriate. There's a child around. And she's just a tiny child but they hear things. And you get careless about it in the beginning and you forget and suddenly she's in kindergarten screaming "fuck" at the teacher. So, just, please. Please, while you're still here.

**BEN**   Don't touch the baseboards tonight, okay?

**JACKIE**   You understand about your language, the spirit it's meant in?

**BEN**  It's my last day anyway.

**JACKIE**  Today then. Please.

**BEN**  And who said "fuck"? I said "jerking off."

*Ben goes into the house.*

**JACKIE**  And if you could leave your keys.

**BEN** (*from inside*)  I never had keys.

**JACKIE**  Of course you had keys.

**BEN** (*from inside*)  No, someone was always letting me in.

*Jackie looks down the drive one more time. He goes into the house momentarily and returns with a cordless phone. He is about to make a call when* JOYCE, *a middle-aged woman, enters. She wears sunglasses and carries a shoulder bag.*

**JOYCE**  There was traffic.

**JACKIE**  I probably didn't mention how long my commute is.

**JOYCE**  I was thinking that.

**JACKIE**  My fault, I probably didn't mention it.

**JOYCE**  No, you did.

**JACKIE**  In all the craziness—

**JOYCE**  You did, you mentioned it's long and I was thinking by being late I'm making his commute that much longer.

**JACKIE**  I'm probably right in the thick of it now.

**JOYCE**  You should call.

**JACKIE**  Probably right in it.

**JOYCE**  You should call your boss and say you're behind so your boss will know, and you should go in ten minutes to avoid the rush.

*Jackie takes the phone into the house. Joyce puts her things down, takes off her sunglasses and looks at the child. Ben returns to the yard, this time with paint cans, rollers, etc.*

**JOYCE**  Hello.

*Ben goes down the drive without replying. Joyce ponders the child. Jackie returns from the house with the phone, which he sets on the lawn chair.*

**JACKIE**  I called. Thank you. It turns out the meeting's been pushed back. So I'm okay. (*beat*) I'm okay.

*They ponder the child together.*

**JOYCE**  She's sleeping. How long does she sleep?

**JACKIE**  Quite a bit. We've had her checked, though. She's fine.

*They ponder the child again.*

**JACKIE** (*cont.*)  She's really perfectly fine.

**JOYCE**  She shouldn't roll on her stomach.

**JACKIE**  I don't think she can do that.

**JOYCE**  Sometimes if you turn or get distracted, they can roll on their stomachs.

**JACKIE**  She hasn't done that yet.

**JOYCE**  They can learn that in a day. One day you say they can't, they don't have the strength, the next day they're like seals—flipping, flopping.

**JACKIE**  We haven't seen any flipping. (*beat*) I keep saying "we."

*There is a silence.*

**JOYCE**  And the boy with the paint?

**JACKIE**  It's his last day. He's coming and going. You can ignore him.

**JOYCE**  What if the neighbors visit?

**JACKIE**  They don't. Mrs. Barnes does sometimes. She'll bring something. Dessert, cupcakes. Just say thank you and don't engage her. She'll be your best friend and then it's all over. She'll be here twenty-four/seven. And we don't like her. Her kitchen window looks into our kitchen window and she's retired and we're not friends. So she stands at the window waiting for when we pass. She stands there washing dishes all day. How many dishes can a retired old lady wash? She lives by herself, her kids are in Florida. She got all involved and they didn't want it. Two are on drugs. You hear through neighbors. (*beat*) Okay, is everything in order?

**JOYCE**  I'm not sure. I feel suddenly not sure.

**JACKIE**  Just always refer to your list.

*Joyce takes a list from her bag.*

**JOYCE**  We went through it.

**JACKIE**  The names, the contacts—when I called last night everything was fine.

**JOYCE**  I checked off things, I did.

**JACKIE**  You had everything straight.

**JOYCE**  You want to be sure, to double-check. Names, contacts—

**JACKIE**  You're fine. It's nothing.

*Joyce checks her list.*

**JOYCE**  I think I have everything. I think I know everything. Emergency phone numbers?

**JACKIE**  That's all written down in the kitchen. On a piece of yellow pad paper. A piece that hangs by the door. There's fire, police, hospital—

**JOYCE**  Fire, police, hospital.

**JACKIE**  Poison centers. The closest ones.

**JOYCE**  Poison centers—smart. The closest poison centers is very smart.

**JACKIE**  The gas and electric if you smell anything.

**JOYCE**  But Jackie, you can't smell gas.

**JACKIE**  Some gas you can.

**JOYCE**  No, that's the thing, it's odorless and envelops you.

**JACKIE**  Then everyone will die. (*beat*) I'm sorry.

**JOYCE**  No, I understand that's funny. And the bassinet's okay on the ground, that's fine?

**JACKIE**  It's a cool surface underneath. We found a cool surface is best. And the new central air in the house still isn't working. So the house is, at the moment, moist.

**JOYCE**  Moist, like humid?

**JACKIE**  It's humid and the moistness makes for mold and the baby is allergic. To the house. Sneezing, screaming, sneezing, screaming.

**JOYCE**  Poor thing.

**JACKIE**  Mold spores.

**JOYCE**  Mold spores.

**JACKIE**  Little spores. So if you wouldn't mind staying outside?

*Ben returns from the drive and heads for the house.*

**JOYCE**  The great outdoors. Not at all.

**BEN**  Alfresco. (*Ben goes into the house.*)

**JACKIE**  Okay. I should get going. (*He starts to go.*)

**JOYCE**  Yesterday I got a letter. From Pam.

*Jackie stops. Joyce takes the letter from her bag.*

**JOYCE** (*cont.*)  I thought it was odd. I hardly know her. And it said I hope you know I'm not a bad mother. She says she's writing everyone. I don't know who all that is. Who that includes. I don't know if you'll be "everyone." It says the last thing she'd want to be is not a good mother. The very last thing. It breaks her heart. A little baby. A mother gone. What people think. (*She offers the letter to Jackie and he takes it.*)

**JOYCE** (*cont.*)  It says she's from a family of boys. But she wanted a girl and she got one. (*beat*) I forgot my mints in the car.

*Joyce goes down the drive. Jackie reads the letter and cries. Joyce returns on the drive with her candies.*

**JOYCE** (*cont.*)  Pastilles, not mints.

*Jackie returns Pam's letter to Joyce.*

**JOYCE** (*cont.*)  I need to wash my hands.

**JACKIE**  Please wash your hands and then I'm off.

186

*Joyce goes inside. From his jacket, Jackie withdraws a handheld tape recorder, which he speaks into.*

**JACKIE** *(cont.)*  Letter to Pam. Dear Pam. I understand you're writing people. Don't. And don't expect understanding. When you finally show up. Whenever I bring this up to people they are appalled. Appalled. Who do you think you are? Running off without warning? I can't bring it up to everyone for the baby's sake—for your sake. I'm protecting you from people's thoughts. Their judgments, which are harsh. People think all kinds of mean and vicious things when a mother leaves—and why shouldn't it reflect on you when you don't know what you're doing! You can't know. What I feel. Which is loss. *(beat)* Were you outside last night? Wherever you're staying? The moon was full. I know you like that. *(beat)* In closing. The baby's fine. All bundled up and different every day. Your catalogues are piling up. From all those stores. I'm saving them for you. I don't know if I should. *(beat)* Maybe I should throw them out. *(beat)* Maybe I should just throw that shit out!

*Joyce returns from the house and sees Jackie's recorder.*

**JOYCE**  I didn't know if you got it.

**JACKIE**  I meant to send a note.

**JOYCE**  And you use it?

**JACKIE**  Reminders. Gentle reminders. Okay, did you wash your hands?

**JOYCE**  The hands are washed.

**JACKIE**  Good. And so if that's everything—is that everything?

**JOYCE**  Can I bring the TV out?

JACKIE  Uh—

JOYCE  In the afternoons, when she's sleeping. And I was thinking of calling one of my old girlfriends who lives out here. She's a softball coach at the middle school and she's very active. She enjoys visiting people. Cynthia Faunstauver. She was in my wedding. Third bridesmaid down. She would've been closer but she said something at my shower.

JACKIE  I'm not supposed to have a lot of people over.

JOYCE  Just Cynthia Faunstauver.

JACKIE  Strangers. I've been advised there should only be friends.

JOYCE  But Cynthia Faunstauver?

JACKIE  Friends or family only, really.

JOYCE  You remember Cynthia.

JACKIE  Strangers milling about isn't good, if there's a fight, a custody fight, neighbors talk and if they saw people—

JOYCE  Cynthia, from the old days?

JACKIE  —and if I need character witnesses—

JOYCE  A bridesmaid at my wedding!

JACKIE  I was six at your wedding!

JOYCE  Six-year-olds have memories!

*They are silent a moment. And Ben appears briefly in the upstairs window.*

JACKIE  I just think the whole thing's a little much.

**JOYCE**  Fine.

**JACKIE**  The next thing you know you'll want little get-togethers here.

**JOYCE**  What little get-togethers?

**JACKIE**  Little get-togethers older people have. And if I say yes to one bridesmaid you might want others. Okay when I'm here, maybe, sometime, once, one person can come over. Someone I know. I really don't remember this softball coach bridesmaid.

**JOYCE**  She was in my wedding, she did the catering, she made an ice sculpture. A swan on top of where the shrimp were. She's perfectly harmless.

**JACKIE**  The memory of a six-year-old is selective. (*beat*) So just whoever's on your list.

**JOYCE**  Of course. Whatever you want. Whatever.

*A moment passes.*

**JOYCE**  And when do I turn the sprinklers on?

**JACKIE**  Don't touch them, I'm the only one to touch them. It's just they're on a timer and they're temperamental. And the slightest misarrangement sets them off. And it's suddenly a spectacular water show.

**JOYCE**  So many regulations.

**JACKIE**  It's just, I would like to see if this could work out. (*beat*) If it works for a more—on a more permanent basis.

**JOYCE**  Me?

**JACKIE**  Sitting with the baby on a more permanent basis.

**JOYCE**    An arrangement?

**JACKIE**    That's what we'll see. If my current situation continues. If Pam continues to be missing.

**JOYCE**    Jackie.

**JACKIE**    If Pam continues to be elsewhere.

**JOYCE**    A permanent basis.

*A moment passes in silence.*

**JACKIE**    Okay, if that's everything, I'm off. Is that everything? The towels, the numbers, the contacts, the clean diapers, the schedule of times, feeding, naps—feeding, naps—pick her up every now and then, play with the brightly colored keys, make words or don't—I'm back at six. Six or so. Feeding, naps, diapers, fire, police, poison. Sometimes earlier if there's a break. Five, five-thirty.

**JOYCE**    That's it.

**JACKIE**    Six, six-thirty, latest. And you don't have to pick up the phone. Let the machine get it.

**JOYCE**    I'll let the machine.

**JACKIE**    Not that you're not capable.

**JOYCE**    Of course!

**JACKIE**    And please don't make food or dust. And if you use the phone be careful. The last time you were over there was some kind of sticky stuff all over it.

**JOYCE**    I believe I'd had some gummy bears.

**JACKIE**    That reminds me, please don't give the baby what's not on that list. Gummy bears or other things. There's an infant diet to adhere to. For children who can't tolerate certain foods.

**JOYCE**  Well, infants can't tolerate gummy bears.

**JACKIE**  I'm just saying.

**JOYCE**  An infant with gummy bears? They'd lodge in a child's esophagus. I've read that anything larger than the size of a thumb is too large for a child's esophagus.

**JACKIE**  Just what every father wants to hear. I'm sorry.

**JOYCE**  No, that's funny too, I know. Anything else?

**JACKIE**  No, nothing. Please don't alphabetize anything.

**JOYCE**  For Christ's sake!

**JACKIE**  I'm sorry.

**JOYCE**  Don't worry!

**JACKIE**  I'm not.

**JOYCE**  I feel needed.

**JACKIE**  You are.

**JOYCE**  Good. Good.

**JACKIE**  Everything's unsettled.

**JOYCE**  I know.

**JACKIE**  We have to look at this current situation as an extraordinary time. When I've saved enough for day care, things will be different.

**JOYCE**  So that's the future.

**JACKIE**  This caught me off guard.

**JOYCE**   The present tends to. For everyone. (*beat*) Extraordinary. It is. (*beat*) Jackie. Your father's face.

**JACKIE**   I'll see what I can do. About your bridesmaid friend. But only the one who plays softball. I'll see what's possible.

**JOYCE**   We all will.

**JACKIE**   Good then, I'm off.

**JOYCE**   The memorial service has been scheduled for two weeks from yesterday. That's the half-year anniversary.

**JACKIE**   Right.

**JOYCE**   You said you'd speak. Some words about your father. Ten minutes tops.

**JACKIE**   Sure.

**JOYCE**   We want to keep it short. I want to keep it short. I still say "we" too. Now we're "we." Us.

*A moment passes.*

**JOYCE** *(cont.)*   Jackie, this will work out.

**JACKIE**   Okay. (*He starts to go*)

**JOYCE**   Well, say good-bye to the baby.

**JACKIE**   She doesn't need a lot of handling. I won't disturb her.

*As Jackie goes, he takes his mini-recorder and speaks into it.*

**JACKIE** *(cont.)*   Notes for Dad's service. Mention clubs and organizations, hobbies in later years: origami, football pool, wood carving in the garage—

*And he's gone.*

**JOYCE**  Your father's going. (*beat*) Wave goodbye to your father . . .

*When Jackie's car is heard pulling onto the street, Joyce checks the baby. Finding the brightly colored keys, she halfheartedly plays with them. Finally, she sits down. She looks around and realizes there is nothing to do. Remembering something in her bag, she withdraws a package of gummy bears, which she dips into. She grabs the phone to make a call and then realizes what she's done. She takes one of the baby's diaper wipes and cleans the phone meticulously. When finished, she stares straight ahead.*

**JOYCE**  Names, contacts. Fire, police. Fire, police, poison. Poison centers. Smart. Yellow paper in kitchen. Yellow pad paper. Allergic. Alfresco. Clean diapers. Brightly colored keys. Make words. Words.

*And then she remembers something else in her bag. She rummages in it and withdraws a handheld tape recorder, exactly like Jackie's. She thinks about what she might say into it, then clicks it on.*

**JOYCE** (*cont.*)  Draft of holiday slash New Year's letter. Draft one—July. Please excuse the form of this letter as during the busy holiday time, cetra, et cetera, I am unable to write each of you with a personalized cetra, cetra, et cetera. (*she thinks*) Another year come and gone. We've had more ups and downs than anticipated. Note to self: see synonyms for roller coaster. Continuing: I've been baby-sitting Margueretta now for . . . mmm . . . it will be . . . by then . . . six months. It's been an arrangement that started in July at my recommendation and now she's a full . . . three months now so . . . nine months old by New Year's. I'm glad and surprised Jackie took me up on the offer, as we've always had our . . . uh . . . rough patches since I married his father. Note to self: rephrase previous sentence more diplomatically. Continuing: but when a child is involved, adults can sometimes come together. Which is good! (*she looks at the child*) Margueretta. Named after Pam's mother's. Margy. With a hard G. Grandma Margy lives far away and isn't really a part of the picture. But grandmothers come in many packages and don't need to be right next door. Note to self: X last sentence. But she's an attentive grandma, sending cards whenever she can. Parentheses— infrequently. A little irreverence for my very close friends. Close parentheses. Continuing: even though Pam and Jackie are still separated, we have high hopes. Alternate sentence: Pam and Jackie are now back together after their trial separation. Hooray for love. We are all relieved to be facing the new year together. (*beat*) Mostly together. This year we lost Jackie Senior. To something the doctors couldn't explain. And life is different. Apparently this happens all the time. People die suddenly in spite of medical advances. Friends say I'll get used to it. This loss. I don't believe them. I don't believe them! (*beat*) What do friends know about being lonely?

*After a moment the phone rings. Joyce is startled and moves to it quickly. But she isn't looking where she's going and she topples the bassinet. The baby cries, but only for a brief moment.*

**JOYCE** (*cont.*)   God!

*Joyce rights the bassinet and sits, recovering herself. Several moments pass before* TED, *a man of about forty, comes into the yard with a Weedwacker. He doesn't see Joyce as he starts mowing the edge of the lawn.*

**JOYCE**   You can't mow near a baby!

**TED**   It's the third Thursday of the month.

**JOYCE**   You can't mow near a baby!

*Ben appears in the window upstairs. Ted turns off the Weedwacker.*

194

**TED**  Do you have my check?

*Joyce doesn't answer.*

**TED** *(cont.)*  Are you Margy?

**BEN**  We're not allowed to talk.

**JOYCE**  I'm certainly not Margy, Margy lives far away.

**BEN**  Do you know Pam?

**JOYCE**  Please.

**TED**  I deal with Jackie.

**BEN**  Pam's his wife. She's missing.

**JOYCE**  Please!

**TED**  I figured something went wrong when I stopped seeing her car.

**JOYCE**  None of us should be talking.

*Ben withdraws from the window.*

**TED**  I'm from two houses down and I drive by and her car's been gone.

*Again, Joyce does not answer him. She puts on her sunglasses and sits. Ted starts to go.*

**JOYCE**  There's no return address on her letters but the postmark says Fairmount Heights.

*Ted stops.*

**TED** *(cont.)*  Can't you take the baby inside?

**JOYCE**  There's a mold spore issue.

*Ted takes out a cigarette.*

**TED**  Fairmount Heights, huh? Lots of single people in the Heights. Bars and restaurants that cater to a single clientele. It's where young people go to meet prospective mates. (*Ted lights his cigarette.*)

**JOYCE**  I'm sure she's not off being single. Certainly not "carefree" single. I think she's probably off being, well, subdued single. She's a wife and mother, even if she isn't around.

**TED**  Maybe she's on a singles cruise.

**JOYCE**  We really shouldn't be talking.

*But Ted doesn't move to go.*

**JOYCE** (*cont.*)  Why would her letters be postmarked Fairmount Heights if she's floating over the Caribbean somewhere?

**TED**  She can mail the letters to a friend in the Heights, in an envelope, a manila envelope and the friend can dump the contents of the envelope in the mailbox. That's how kidnappers work. (*beat*) I'm thinking about taking one of those cruises. You can meet people. One of those cruises where meals are included. It seems like a big price tag but when you factor in all the extras: the buffet, the entertainment, the open bar at cocktail hour. The view alone! The water, the open sea. The beds—the berths, exercise on the Lido Deck. I'd exercise on a vacation. Why not keep yourself up? You might be on vacation but gravity's not. And he didn't leave a check?

**JOYCE**  I'm really kept in the dark.

**TED**  With every check I put some aside.

**JOYCE**  I do that too.

**TED**  A cruise costs money.

**JOYCE**  Except with me there's no cruise—like you have your cruise, your goal of a cruise—my money aside is just aside. I like to think of it. Sitting securely in a bank. Stacked neatly with a rubber band. In case things go terribly wrong.

**TED**  It's not real money.

**JOYCE**  Excuse me?

**TED**  It's just numbers next to your name that correspond to the Federal Reserve. They don't have a pile of your money at the bank in a room. It's not like it's a wad of cash in a room somewhere with your name on it!

**JOYCE**  Yes, I get it.

**TED**  (*beat*)  I have a complimentary videotape of all the cruises. The specifics of each one, what they offer. I bet there's one for you.

**JOYCE**  I'm not big on water.

**TED**  Half the time you don't even know you're on water!

**JOYCE**  I don't like fish, even.

**TED**  You never see fish! And the menus include other things beside fish. They include pasta bars. Design your own pasta. Carving tables, ice cream stations.

**JOYCE**  Just the thought of fish and water and all that food makes me crazy! (*beat*) I do like rigatoni.

**TED**  You tell Jackie I was here and there was no check and you wouldn't let me work, see what he says. He should contact me like a gentleman if he no longer wants my services.

*He takes out his wallet and hands her his card. She takes off her sunglasses.*

**JOYCE**  You understand I don't want to do anything that could get either of us in trouble.

**TED**  I come every third Thursday in summer—

**JOYCE**  Unscheduled mowing—

**TED**  —So I don't get it.

**JOYCE**  But just who are you?

**TED**  It's on the card.

*She looks at his name and then checks it against her list.*

**JOYCE**  You're not on the list. He's very particular is all, and I don't want to step out of bounds. He's tough on the people around him. I don't mind. He's the man now. Since my husband died. And our friends have slipped away. We shared friends, couples, my husband and me, and now they're all embarrassed that he's dead. Or something. Do you have an extra cigarette?

*He offers her a cigarette and lights it for her.*

**JOYCE** *(cont.)*  Thank you. (*looks at his card*) Ted. For the (*reads the cigarette*) Winston. I don't understand people. You seem nice.

**TED**  I'm okay.

**JOYCE**  Good head on your shoulders.

**TED**  I work at it.

**JOYCE**  Friendships on cruises. I do understand Jackie, though. We're just alike.

**TED**  That's nice.

**JOYCE**   It is. He's complicated. He's narcoleptic. Most people don't know. He's regulated it with his diet. By reducing his starches. And thank God. Sleep coming on at the most unexpected times. There are other things too. That complicate him.

**TED**   It's good he has you.

**JOYCE**   I know all about him. We're really very close, Ted, Jackie and I. A special understanding that goes unsaid.

**TED**   You seem nice too.

**JOYCE**   I'm not, I'm mean. Lonely people are never nice. (*beat*) I'm not lonely now. It would be nice to stay this way.

**TED**   I've got ten minutes.

**JOYCE**   You're not on the list.

**TED**   There must be names he's forgotten.

*They smoke a bit in silence.*

**JOYCE**   So people have affairs on these cruises?

**TED**   It's practically guaranteed. There was a *60 Minutes* special on widespread sex on boats at sea. Unbelievable. The crew can get in trouble, though. They're supposed to be platonic.

**JOYCE**   I just want you to know, Ted, in case you're thinking things—I love my husband. Even though he's gone. I don't know if I'm ready for anything. Just yet.

**TED**   No, no.

**JOYCE**   Oh—okay.

**TED**   No, no.

**JOYCE**   Good.

**TED**   Under the circumstances.

**JOYCE**   Yes.

**TED**   Things are complicated enough.

**JOYCE**   My God, it's true!

**TED**   Even though you're an attractive woman.

**JOYCE**   I'm flattered.

**TED**   If things were different—

**JOYCE**   And they're not. They are not.

**TED**   And you're an attractive woman.

**JOYCE**   It's nice to hear. Nonetheless. Nonetheless.

*They smoke a moment in silence.*

**TED**   And I like women, I do.

**JOYCE**   Yes. Who doesn't?

**TED**   I'm not exclusively with men. And I can say that, no problem. I mean, why should saying that be a problem?

**JOYCE**   I don't know.

**TED**   People come in all kinds.

**JOYCE**   They do, they really do.

**TED**   That's why me and Jackie got along. Even though it complicates things and that's why we stopped the minute it started. Even though Pam was gone when it happened, it was something I would not pursue when people are married. (*beat*) That's why I'm researching these cruises.

**JOYCE**   I don't know what you're saying, Ted.

*The doorbell rings repeatedly from the front of the house. Joyce goes into the house to answer it. While she's gone, Ben appears in the upstairs window. He is scrutinizing* ted *when Joyce returns. Ben moves away from the window.*

**JOYCE**   U.P.S.

**TED**   You said you knew about Jackie.

**JOYCE**   We've been out of touch.

**TED**   You two are close.

**JOYCE**   I meant I knew how his mind worked.

**TED**   Oh, Christ.

**JOYCE**   He resents me.

**TED**   Oh, Christ, fuck.

**JOYCE**   I married in. We're not close.

**TED**   Oh, Christ, fuck, fuck.

**JOYCE**   I'm his father's wife.

**TED**   Son of a fucking Christ!

**JOYCE**   His father's wife. How could I know that?

**TED**   I wasn't here.

*The baby cries.*

**JOYCE**   Her bottle . . . ?

**TED**   We never talked.

**JOYCE**   Of course.

**TED**   And he's a good man.

**JOYCE**  I know.

**TED**  And I—live alone.

**JOYCE**  You're a neighbor two houses down and we never talked.

**TED**  If anyone says I was here we talked about nothing. We talked about the baby. Something about her. How cute she is, hungry, the bruises they get.

*Joyce looks at the child.*

**JOYCE**  Just before you came I toppled the bassinet. (*she sees something*) A bruise. There is one.

*Ben comes from the house with a pitcher of lemonade and two glasses.*

**BEN**  I'm almost done packing up so I made some lemonade. Sometimes Pam let me put a shot in it. Tequila? Then it's called "electric lemonade." I know it's only ten A.M., but it's drinking time somewhere! Huh or what?

*Ted and Joyce look at each other.*

**TED**  Kids are resilient.

**JOYCE**  We should all be resilient.

*Ted goes down the drive. Joyce puts on her sunglasses and sits. Ben settles in at her side and they drink together, glass after glass of "electric lemonade," as the morning light becomes late afternoon light, and Mrs. Barnes sends a plate of cupcakes over the fence, followed by a Jell-o mold. Ben retrieves the offerings and, eventually, the baby cries. Joyce does not move. So Ben picks up the baby's bottle and starts feeding her. It is now 6:00.*

**BEN**  I love Pam. I wish she'd come back. If only because you want people you love to come back. When they're elsewhere it sucks. (*beat*) I love her body. That's not why I love her. Her body. Though it could be. Pam is stacked. And why can't that be why to be in love? Love is pleasure! Love is pleasure—why can't a kid hear that? (*to the baby*) You aren't gonna scream "fuck" in kindergarten. (*to Joyce*) I know what kids say and when they start saying it. Second grade is when "fuck" is first uttered. (*to the baby*) Yeah, I love your mother and I have what she needs. (*to Joyce*) Which is energy. She's always tired and I'm like what's with that? Don't be tired—that's the answer. But sometimes you need someone else's energy to recharge your own. See, we're batteries! But Jackie doesn't have energy. I'm not saying mean things about Jackie—he's okay, he's just tired. Why can't I say that around the baby? She'll know it in, like, ten months. She'll be aware of an extremely exhausted father. And I'm all about the opposite of exhaustion, which is possibility, what's next! It's like I'm on fire—there's no prescribed plan. (*beat*) I put my head in Pam's lap once. She hardly knew it. She kept talking, then lifted it up with her hands, which smelled like something lemony fresh. She went out through the screen door and the sun went through her blouse. Which is not why I'm in love. Though why couldn't it be? (*beat*) She let me kiss her once. But on the forehead. So, you know, no tongue or anything. Which sucks, 'cause tongue rocks. But just as well, 'cause she was crying at the sink. Which is, I've noticed, where women tend to cry.

**JOYCE**   I'm not supposed to talk to anybody.

*After a moment, Jackie's car is heard in the drive. Ben scrambles to take the lemonade and Mrs. Barnes's desserts into the house. Joyce collects her things and stands, ready to go, as Jackie comes into the yard with a shopping bag.*

**JACKIE**   So. How'd it go?

**JOYCE**   Fine. Nothing. She slept. She fussed a bit.

**JACKIE**   She was hungry.

**JOYCE**   She only fussed a little. She's teething maybe.

**JACKIE**   All babies fuss.

**JOYCE**   She's an angel. She really is. But now I'm late.

**JACKIE**   So everything went fine?

**JOYCE**   Like clockwork.

**JACKIE**   Good! Great. And the boy painting?

**JOYCE**   Almost finished. No bother. Came and went.

**JACKIE**   And Mrs. Barnes?

**JOYCE**   Cupcakes and Jell-o.

**JACKIE**   Unbelievable! She came in the yard?

**JOYCE**   Only to the fence.

**JACKIE**   How did you handle it?

**JOYCE**   I hardly said anything. Just pleasantries.

**JACKIE**   Good.

**JOYCE**   She tried to engage me and I would not have it. I
indicated I had things to do. I changed the tone in my
voice. You would've been proud.

**JACKIE**   I am. I really am. Is something wrong?

**JOYCE**   I was thinking I should get on my way before traffic
hits. I want to go to El Pollo Grande before they close.
They make a lovely chimichanga I like. (*She starts to go.*)

**JACKIE**   I brought some beer. If you want one.

**JOYCE**   El Pollo Grande runs out of white meat by seven.

**JACKIE**   We could order in? There number's somewhere and I got all different ones. I don't know what you like.

*Jackie chooses a beer for Joyce.*

**JOYCE**   We don't have an opener.

*Jackie has an opener on his key chain and opens the two beers, handing one to Joyce. A moment passes.*

**JACKIE**   I'll keep them in the fridge. If you ever want one. There's nothing wrong with having a beer in the summer, during the day.

*They sip their beer.*

**JACKIE** (*cont.*)   And there's nothing wrong?

**JOYCE**   Everything's fine. (*beat*) This is a big beer.

**JACKIE**   It's the shape of the bottle.

**JOYCE**   I probably won't have time to finish it. (*She reads the label on the beer.*) Pale ale. What's that?

**JACKIE**   It's an ale that's . . . not dark.

**JOYCE**   It's pale.

**JACKIE** (*beat*)   This is nice. We don't do this. You and me. Some beer. A chat.

**JOYCE**   No, we don't.

**JACKIE**   Well, since you're a part of things now.

**JOYCE**   Yes.

**JACKIE**   After some time.

**JOYCE**   For some time I haven't been, no. And now I am.

**JACKIE**  And I want to thank you.

**JOYCE**  Please don't.

**JACKIE**  No, really. I'm making headway on my speech. (*he takes his mini-recorder from his pocket*) It helps having Dad's recorder. Holding the recorder he held. Thanks for thinking of me with it. (*beat*) I was thinking also what you said before. (*beat*) That now we're "we."

*Another moment passes in silence.*

**JOYCE**  There was a package that came. Something someone ordered. From a company. I signed for it. An appliance, apparently. Pam, probably. Things take weeks to arrive. On the top was taped a catalogue of other things to order for your house.

**JACKIE**  All those catalogues.

**JOYCE**  Indoor, outdoor things.

**JACKIE**  Clogging the mailbox.

**JOYCE**  I didn't look at it.

**JACKIE**  You could have.

**JOYCE**  I don't want to be where I shouldn't.

**JACKIE**  Our catalogues are your catalogues.

**JOYCE**  That's the only other person who came by—after Mrs. Barnes and the boy painting. A U.P.S. girl. It's a nice uniform. Brown. (*beat*) I heard the mailman at one point. But didn't see him. (*beat*) The phone rang, but don't worry. (*beat*) I should really get on the road before it's crazy. (*She starts to go.*)

**JACKIE**  But Pam's coming. She faxed me at work.

**JOYCE** (*beat*)  She's coming here?

**JACKIE**  She's coming.

**JOYCE**  This whole time she's been coming?

*Jackie takes the fax from his pocket and offers it to Joyce. She does not take it.*

**JACKIE**  It says before dinner. But no time. No specific time.

**JOYCE**  Before dinner could mean anytime.

**JACKIE**  When we had dinner is what she means, is what I'm thinking. Five-thirty, six. Five, five-thirty, six. The latest six, six-thirty.

**JOYCE**  That's now.

**JACKIE**  Now-ish.

*Ben enters from the house.*

**JOYCE**  I should go.

**JACKIE**  Please don't.

**JOYCE**  I hardly know Pam.

**JACKIE**  I wish you wouldn't.

**JOYCE**  Well, everyone would admit I hardly know Pam.

**BEN**  She's excellent.

**JACKIE**  I could pay you.

**JOYCE**  Please!

**JACKIE**  The extra time.

**JOYCE**  Really, please.

*Jackie goes into the house and returns with a stack of Pam's catalogues, which he hands to Joyce. He indicates that she should sit.*

**JACKIE**   What you said before. What you said. Who we are now.

*Joyce sits slowly and opens one of the catalogues. Jackie turns to Ben.*

**JACKIE**   Shouldn't you be done by now?

**BEN**   My brushes are still soaking.

**JACKIE**   Okay, when Pam comes everyone has to go inside. And if she stays, then everyone should go home. If she doesn't stay, everyone can stay or go or do what they want.

*As they wait for Pam, Jackie begins to pace in a circle around the yard. Ben moves to stand by the drive. And Joyce pages through Pam's catalogues. After a moment, Jackie looks over Joyce's shoulder.*

**JACKIE**   That's interesting. What's that one?

**JOYCE**   Yard items.

**JACKIE**   Could you read some of that?

**JOYCE**   Aloud?

**JACKIE**   Like we're just here and we're doing things.

**JOYCE**   Reading to each other?

**JACKIE**   Let's just keep going about things. (*beat*) So this is good. We should be like we are. And she'll be here soon, so we won't have to do it for long.

*After a moment Joyce begins to read aloud from the catalogue.*

**JOYCE**   "Built to endure, teakwood trunks provide long-lasting storage—and beauty—outdoors."

**JACKIE** (*beat*)   Dinner was usually five, five-thirty, so she should be here soon.

**JOYCE**   "Displayed as sculptures or fountains, these copper seagulls beautify any outdoor setting."

**JACKIE** (*beat*)   Five, five-thirty, six.

**JOYCE**   "This umbrella moves with the sun so you don't have to." (*beat*) "Hand-finished all-weather terra-cotta African clocks with put-me-anywhere versatility."

**JACKIE** (*beat*)   Six, six-thirty, latest.

**JOYCE**   "Large, lifelike bronze turtle and snail sculptures command notice. Peering from among the ferns or pausing as they inch their way across the coffee table, these two slowpokes are reminders of life lived at a more leisurely pace." Well. We can certainly learn from animals.

**JACKIE** (*beat*)   Maybe where she's living there's a fax machine. Or where she's working. They say she's out when I call. She might have a home fax. Wherever she's staying. That would interest her.

**BEN** (*beat*)   I fixed her fax once.

**JOYCE** (*beat*)   "Our multitiered occasional table is a profusion of color and charm. When the setting calls for an eye-catching accent, what more could you ask for than this captivating table?" Well, I just don't know.

**JACKIE**   What?

**JOYCE**   Jackie?

**JACKIE**   Please.

*There is a long silence.*

**JACKIE** (*cont.*) It's not really before dinner any longer. I know.

**BEN** It wasn't even any longer ten minutes ago, even. It wasn't.

**JACKIE** What did I do? (*beat*) The thing I don't get is what did I do? You know? (*beat*) It's a two-way street. She's part of it. A few late nights! My friends over—and hardly ever. Hardly ever except Phil Miyale—who is a friend from college! Nothing was different. Nothing! (*beat*) She didn't like this one gift I wanted to give my Secret Santa. Inappropriate or something. This little ceramic thing. She's like, "It's not funny." Why did I even show her? She's like, "He won't get it." I knew the taste of my Secret Santa. Working on that account seven months and I don't know his taste? She's like, "People who have lupus don't like jokey gifts!" She's all the time here—she wasn't in my workforce, my environment. She had her own environment. Lupus isn't even always fatal! He's had it thirteen years! He didn't laugh at cheap jokes for thirteen years because of lupus? You learn to live with things. You better laugh or you just don't. She used to laugh at my jokes. Little teasing. Jokes at each other's expense. She'd laugh and laugh. Until she stopped. The minute she started working at that animal shelter the fun stopped. But then whenever I laughed with someone else, boy oh boy. Sitting there with that face. Stifling anyone else's enjoyment. Standing in the hallway with that face I hated. You just can't be silent with your face! That's why I got the new music system. Liven things up. Our songs! The ones we listened to! They're oldies now but they're good as new on that system! And she's all—she's fucking, "What do we need a new music system for?" Like I'm some ultraconsumer. Fuck you! I would never buy things. Never.

And she's talking about buying? These catalogues? Her tastes were out of hand! Ordering things for the house from catalogues, state-of-the-art kitchen appliances—and who needed a garlic peeler? So your hands don't have to touch garlic! TOUCH SOME GARLIC FOR FUCK'S SAKE!

*There is a silence.*

**BEN**  What *did* you do? (*Ben goes into the house.*)

**JACKIE**  I'd undo it if I knew. I'd undo everything.

**JOYCE**  A person could take her side too, Jackie. What goes through a wife's head.

**JACKIE** (*beat*)  Fine, sure.

**JOYCE**  Suspicions. If I wanted to.

**JACKIE**  Go ahead, fine.

**JOYCE**  I'm not likely to.

**JACKIE**  Take her side, I'd like to see someone make sense of it.

**JOYCE**  I don't—I don't—

**JACKIE**  I would, I really would.

**JOYCE**  Things sometimes happen when a wife is elsewhere.

*There is a short silence.*

**JOYCE** (*cont.*)  Still, we're the ones left—and I don't want to take her side and—we're the ones still where we are. You and me. We didn't go anyplace. No, sir. We had responsibilities we kept! I can't take her side, how could I?

**JACKIE**  What things happen when a wife is elsewhere?

**JOYCE**  Jackie, I've always thought of you as my own and we—

**JACKIE** Something happened?

**JOYCE** —you and I—

**JACKIE** What happens when a wife—

**JOYCE** —we didn't look at life as a series of choices. No, sir. You and I have had obligations and few choices. A baby! The rest of life was for other people! Not Joyce and Jackie Junior!

**JACKIE** Who else was here? When I was at work?

**JOYCE** No one.

**JACKIE** There are cigarettes in the grass.

**JOYCE** The lawn-mower man came for two minutes.

**JACKIE** I canceled that service.

**JOYCE** I sent him away.

**JACKIE** I canceled the lawn service.

**JOYCE** Well, Ted didn't know that. (*beat*) He left his card, it said "Ted."

**JACKIE** And you sat around smoking?

**JOYCE** I'm not kidding about El Pollo Grande and the white meat by seven.

**JACKIE** This isn't working.

**JOYCE** I couldn't get rid of him!

**JACKIE** First Mrs. Barnes—

**JOYCE** I should be off—

**JACKIE** U.P.S., talking with strangers—we didn't discuss this thoroughly. And now we're in a zone we didn't discuss.

**JOYCE**  Just cigarettes!

**JACKIE**  I'll figure something else out, another arrangement—

**JOYCE**  Two minutes with cigarettes—!

**JACKIE**  That's it, it's over!

**JOYCE**  You think you've got it the worst of everyone. At least I married your father after all he went through with your mother! At least I came into the picture for you!

**JACKIE**  Please.

**JOYCE**  At least you get faxes at work! At least you get faxes at work!

*Jackie starts to retrieve the baby's toys, diapers, etc.*

**JOYCE** *(cont.)*  You won't get anyone else for free. You can't afford day care—who will you get? Pam is who knows where—she is who knows where and you're in a bind, mister, that's what this is! No choice. No choice, mister.

**JACKIE**  I'm fairly sure I know of a situation where it's less complicated. Just as inexpensive and less complicated.

**JOYCE**  Not some service.

**JACKIE**  Margy called today. She offered to take care of the baby. As an experiment to see if it might become something more permanent.

**JOYCE** *(beat)*  Margy is miles away.

**JACKIE**  In the meantime.

**JOYCE**  Miles and miles.

**JACKIE**   On a temporary basis. A *different* arrangement! There are choices and I have choices.

**JOYCE**   You can't take the baby to Margy.

*Jackie picks up the baby's bassinet.*

**JOYCE** (*cont.*)   Just today you said—this morning you said a permanent—I have nothing to do sitting in that house— your father's things in boxes—and what am I supposed to do alone in a house with boxes?

*Jackie heads for the house with the baby.*

**JOYCE** (*cont.*)   You can't take the baby to Margy! She doesn't even visit and she only sends cards!

*Jackie is nearing the door.*

**JOYCE** (*cont.*)   I know about Ted. (*beat*) I know about Ted. (*beat*) I wouldn't want to tell Pam. I wouldn't. But from the letter she sent me it's obvious she wants to be in touch with me. Woman to woman. And it's only a matter of time before she sends her return address. Her phone number. And asks for insight. From a woman. And if there's a battle, a custody battle, what I could tell her. Women stick together. Occasionally. In certain instances. This could be one. (*beat*) I'd like to move in for a while.

**JACKIE**   What?

**JOYCE**   Yes. On a temporary basis. When Pam returns this won't ever come up. I'm still on your side.

*A silence passes between them during which Jackie acknowledges he has no choice.*

**JOYCE** (*cont.*)   Then it's settled. I have to wash my hands. Then I'll get set up, upstairs. And tomorrow I'll clean a bit.

I'll tidy. You'll like that. I won't move things around, Jackie, I'll just run a cloth over some things. Yes. And I'll make some food you can heat up. And this fence needs painting and there's a ton of laundry. The towels, the sheets, the rugs are dingy. The curtains, the floors. This is for your own good. Our own good. I feel good, Jackie. For the first time since your father died.

*Jackie returns the bassinet to where it was on the lawn.*

**JOYCE** (*cont.*)   Have you made any headway on your speech?

**BEN** (*calling from inside*)   Who touched the baseboards?

**JOYCE**   You'll see Jackie. We'll be us. We have to be—we're the only ones left.

*Jackie starts down the drive.*

**JOYCE**   Jackie? Are you sure you read Pam's fax correctly? Sometimes they blur.

*Joyce goes down the drive after Jackie and a door in the fence, unseen until now, opens and Pam steps into the yard. She contemplates her child, left alone in the bassinet. The cicada start their sounds . . .*


*End of Act One.*

# ACT TWO

*Later that night. Lawn lanterns have been lit and placed around the yard. Cicadas are heard near and far. The bassinet and baby are still in the yard, as well as some empty beer bottles and a bottle of tequila forgotten in the grass. The television set has been brought to the yard and is plugged into a cord running from the house.*

*Ben is busy painting the back fence. And Joyce, in an apron and rubber gloves for cleaning, has just placed a call. After a moment, her caller picks up.*

**JOYCE**  Hello, is this Cynthia Faunstauver? Cynthia, it's Joyce Tancreedi! Yes, it's Joyce Tancreedi. I can't believe I caught you in! Because I can't believe I caught you in, when you call people no one's ever home anymore! I know! Are you still with the softball at the middle school? Oooo, lacrosse. Well, I'm staying right near you! Yes, 203 Wild Arbor Lane. Yes, 203 Wild Arbor Lane! Well, it's a hop, skip and a fucking jump. I know, I'm sorry—I'm hanging out with young people and I'm cursing all the time now. Yes, I've been saying "shit" too! Now, look, Cynthia, short notice I know, mea culpa, I'm beating myself you can't see, but I'm having a few people over tomorrow. Give a person some warning, right? Well, whoever I can round up of the old group. The before-I-was-married group. (*she listens*) Then you've heard. No, it's just so many people read the obit, so few called. Well, I just thought we could visit. And meet Jackie—Jackie is Jack's boy. It might reflect well on me, my friendship with you, in his eyes. Well, whenever is good, I'm just sitting here all day with the baby. Oh my gosh, yes, we've had a baby! That's why I'm even at 203 Wild Arbor Lane—this is where the baby is! Who is an angel, looking so much like

Jackie, even this early. Her eyes with their questions. Even like my husband's—these two men I know, their eyes, just like them—though she's a girl and I've got that on my side! Don't I, Cynthia? I said she's a girl and—Yes, there's everything to catch up on! Jackie says it's an extraordinary time—and it is, Cynthia. So much! I'll call you in the morning, then. Ta! (*She hangs up and looks around for Ben.*)

**JOYCE** (*cont.*)  Pale ale.

**BEN**  Coming up.

*Ben goes into the house. A flashlight beam comes from the direction of Mrs. Barnes's yard. The light rolls over the ground and comes to rest on Joyce's face.*

**JOYCE**  Go away, Mrs. Barnes.

*But the light remains trained on Joyce.*

**JOYCE** (*cont.*)  Go away!

*The flashlight goes out. While waiting for her pale ale, Joyce takes Ted's business card from her blouse and calls the number. A machine picks up.*

**JOYCE** (*cont.*)  Hello. This is Joyce Tancreedi. We met today. I wouldn't let you mow. I'm leaving a message to say thanks for the Winston cigarette. Even though I'm used to something more mild. The occasional Capri menthol light. Refined tastes. And what good are refined—if—if—look, Ted—I hope this won't click off—but I'm afraid I find myself alone—except for the baby and the boy who paints. He's Ben and he curses and we're friends now—and I'm waiting and with a little booze in me, just beer and tequila, and—and things have gone upside down, have turned and—and—I have what I want for the moment—but I don't know what I'm expected to do. Really. That's the thing of it. How to—to—mother. Or how to handle this situation except take each moment as it comes—since she's looking at me like she maybe needs something and since it's all up in the air anymore—and—let me be clear then. Would you please forgive me if I've said something I shouldn't have? (*beat*) I want to be nice. I do. But also do what's best, what I know to be best, and that is to—to—to, I think, belong. And that is something perhaps we all want. Cruise or no cruise.

*She is cut off by a beep. She hangs up and checks the baby. She wipes something from the baby's face. Jackie comes from the house. He is barefoot and his clothes are rumpled.*

**JOYCE** (*cont.*)   Did Ben wake you?

**JACKIE**   I was working on my speech.

**JOYCE**   He's a loud painter. Chattering.

*Jackie goes to look at the new color on the fence.*

**JOYCE** (*cont.*)   He said you can always go back to the unpainted look. But no matter what, wood needs some kind of treatment. (*beat*) I got some videos. From over the phone. I used your card, your number. I said I was Pam. And they believed me. They delivered them. And cigarettes and popcorn. And I made some food. And left it in the fridge.

**JACKIE**   Where was the baby when you were making food? (*beat*) I'm sorry.

**JOYCE**   I could see her from the window. I had on the walkie-talkie. It's just something you can heat up. If you don't watch your diet the narcolepsy could return. (*beat*) Every day I'll make a little something you can heat up in case you aren't eating.

**JACKIE**   I can cook.

**JOYCE**   You'll be working all day and I'll just be sitting here fending off neighbors. (*beat*) If you want to be alone just say it. Just because we have this arrangement doesn't mean we can't be sensitive. To each other.

**JACKIE**   I don't have narcolepsy anymore.

*Ben returns to the yard with two beers. He hands one to Joyce and resumes painting the fence.*

**JOYCE**   This will take getting used to. A period of adjustment. Practice, even. For when Pam returns. And you're not in the mood for a video? I got several classics. If you change your mind, I'll leave them in the den. (*She moves toward the house.*)

**JACKIE**   Are they classics? Or just old movies?

**JOYCE**   I'm not sure.

**JACKIE**   Someone should determine that. There should be a board somewhere.

**JOYCE**   One is *The Treasure of the Sierra Madre*.

**JACKIE**   There's every chance Pam won't come back. At any point.

*A moment passes and Ben returns to the house.*

**JOYCE**   A movie might do you good. There's popcorn. Which I remember you like.

*Jackie finds a photograph in the grass.*

**JACKIE**   What's this?

*He shows the photo to Joyce.*

**JOYCE**  I was looking at it. The same face, still. The tux made special. A child that age.

*Jackie looks at the photo.*

**JACKIE**  I was imitating a cartoon.

**JOYCE**  Standing like a soldier. I was showing it to Ben. Tiny cuff links. The satin runner.

**JACKIE**  My shoes.

**JOYCE**  The cologne we put on you. An old man's scent. I can smell it. Your slicked hair.

**JACKIE**  Terrible smell. The chapel. The people.

**JOYCE**  Our friends.

**JACKIE**  Eyes and eyes.

**JOYCE**  We were popular. Invitations every weekend, someone's house, cocktails.

**JACKIE**  Adults on either side.

**JOYCE**  Whisky sours. More whisky than sour. All those decanters. I'd pour them.

**JACKIE**  The runner. The aisle.

**JOYCE**  Parties and parties.

**JACKIE**  Both of you at the end of it. Waiting for me.

**JOYCE**  No. The children came first. You, the flower girls. I came the very last. Brides come the last of everyone.

**JACKIE**  Because everyone is longing for her. She will be my new mother.

**JOYCE**  (*beat*) I tried.

**JACKIE**   Our real mother is gone.

*Joyce moves toward him as if she might smooth his hair.*

**JOYCE**   Slicked-back hair.

**JACKIE**   Six-year-olds have memories.

**JOYCE** (*beat*)   A movie might do us both good.

**JACKIE** (*beat*)   Maybe.

**JOYCE**   I'll get Ben to bring the TV in.

**JACKIE**   I should work on my speech.

**JOYCE**   Later, then. (*re: the photograph*) Keep it for the baby. (*beat*) I tried.

*Joyce goes inside. Jackie takes out his mini-recorder and speaks into it.*

**JACKIE**   Notes for Dad's service. Origami. Wood carving. Something . . . in the garage. (*beat*) Origami, carving. Something . . .

*Ted comes on from the drive.*

**TED**   There's a message on my voice mail from this number. I can't retrieve it. It clogged the voice mail. It deactivated it. Sometimes a certain tone of voice will just shut the thing down.

*Ben comes into the yard, lifts the TV in his arms and brings it into the house.*

**TED** (*cont.*)   It's the third Thursday and I came by and no check, nothing. (*Jackie doesn't respond.*) You never said stop the service. I don't care what you think you said. (*Jackie still doesn't respond.*) I would just have appreciated it if you'd told me to my face you no longer need my services.

221

**JACKIE**  Money's been tight.

**TED**  You can't be "the house where the lawn isn't mowed"! I won't stand for that.

**JACKIE**  I'm pretty sure I conveyed—

**TED**  You give me the job back. You give me the job back. No one's gonna cut this grass. You won't.

**JACKIE**  I like to pay as I go.

**TED**  (*beat*)  We should be friends at least. After what happened.

**JACKIE**  I was drunk.

**TED**  Between us. We should be friends.

**JACKIE**  It was nothing.

**TED**  You weren't drunk.

**JACKIE**  It was a mistake. I'm sorry.

**TED**  It wasn't nothing.

**JACKIE**  I love Pam.

**TED**  Don't say "nothing."

**JACKIE**  My child's mother.

**TED**  Don't say "nothing"!

**JACKIE**  My wife! (*Jackie checks to make sure no one is nearby.*) It was four A.M. You were two houses down. Johnny Walker. Shots and shots.

**TED**  You came to my house!

**JACKIE**  Why are people two houses down? People should be far away.

**TED**   You came with a bottle! Don't tell me you didn't come with a bottle.

**JACKIE**   I should be more gentle but it's not a gentle day.

*After a moment, Jackie moves as if he will take the baby inside.*

**TED**   I could watch the baby, then, if you don't need the lawn, and, and—as a friendly thing, a gesture, for when Joyce can't be here. I could take the baby when I do my rounds. I know guys who do it.

**JACKIE**   This isn't everybody's baby! Everybody thinks she's theirs.

**TED**   Joyce can't even handle the baby! She knocked her over. I can handle kids.

**JACKIE**   What—?

**TED**   I'm the oldest of three. I sat for my sisters. Joyce tripped on the kid and she told me. A bruise came up. She is out of touch—and that's who's your sitter?

*Jackie looks at the child and sees a bruise on her forehead.*

**TED** *(cont.)*   You tell me I mean something. You tell me I mean something!

*Joyce enters the yard with a videotape.*

**JOYCE**   We're having some trouble understanding the connection. The cable to the VCR—

**JACKIE**   Please put everything back as it was.

**JOYCE**   Put what back?

**JACKIE**   The sheets, the towels, where you found them.

**JOYCE**   They're in the wash.

223

**JACKIE**   And anything you've rearranged—

**JOYCE**   They're soaking—?

**JACKIE**   —should be—

**JOYCE**   —How dare—

**JACKIE**   —should be—

**JOYCE**   You seem to forget—

**JACKIE**   —rearranged back!

**JOYCE**   You seem to forget—there's something—and this man here—this same person who came today is a person who told me—

**JACKIE**   There's a bruise, Joyce, where there shouldn't be.

**JOYCE**   What?

**JACKIE**   A bruise.

**TED**   You said about when you tripped.

**JOYCE**   What?

**JACKIE**   A bruise.

**JOYCE**   (*beat*)   He came into this yard—immediately mowing—no consideration—

**JACKIE**   As if she'd been dropped.

**TED**   A bruise came up as we talked.

**JOYCE**   Who is this person, Jackie? Who's caused so much—

**JACKIE**   There is a bruise!

**JOYCE**   Babies have all kinds of accidents. Mishaps. They brush against something—or they turn and—and—(*Joyce* *moves to the child and looks at her forehead.*) I did. I tilted the bassinet.

*A moment passes.*

**JACKIE**   Say what you want when Pam gets back.

**JOYCE**   The phone rang right after you left and I wasn't supposed to answer it. And I was running—

**JACKIE**   Tell Pam what you think you know.

**JOYCE**   I was confused and I ran—

**JACKIE**   —or what you invented—

**JOYCE**   I thought maybe it was—

**JACKIE**   —in desperation.

**JOYCE**   —Pam or someone important—

**JACKIE**   To cover up your incompetence.

**JOYCE**   —or some news—

**JACKIE**   Incompetence.

**TED**   Come on, Jackie.

**JOYCE**   The phone rang and did it ever occur to you it could be good news? Good news I wasn't allowed to receive? All your rules and it could be good news you're ignoring!

**JACKIE**   Your incompetence.

**JOYCE**   You can't be incompetent in a job you never wanted! I wanted to be married! I didn't want children! I wanted to be a newlywed and you were in my way!

*There is a long silence.*

**JOYCE** (*cont.*)  I need to wash my hands. And then I should get on the road.

**JACKIE**  Yes, don't you have a chicken deadline?

**JOYCE**  What? Oh. Sometimes they don't run out. That's only—

*Once again, the flashlight shines from Mrs. Barnes's yard.*

**JOYCE**  That's only on nights when they've had an unexpectedly huge turnout. If there's a convention. Or a parade.

*The flashlight passes back and forth over Jackie's yard.*

**JOYCE** (*cont.*)  Your father would know, always up on those things. (*beat*) Everyone thinks I'm nice. (*beat*) I'll return the video. On my way.

*The light continues to roam the space.*

**JOYCE** (*cont.*)  Go back to bed, Mrs. Barnes! Your children are on drugs in Florida!

*The beam from the flashlight is stilled a moment and then turned off.*

**JOYCE** (*cont.*)  I'll just wash my hands and go. This is, apparently, no longer a permanent situation.

*Joyce goes into the house.*

**TED**  It's not fair, Jackie.

**JACKIE**  After tonight, we'll nod over the hedges. Most neighbors nod over hedges. (*Jackie goes to pick up the baby. And again, he cannot.*)

**TED**  I want you to think about me watching the baby. I sat for my sisters. I work out of my house. You come home at night. Who knows when Pam's coming back? I live alone. And I don't want to.

**JACKIE**  Ted?

**TED**  Yeah, Jackie.

**JACKIE**  What's happening? To everything? I don't recognize anything.

**TED**  I'm telling you, people should be together.

**JACKIE**  I'm even losing track of time. The weeks.

**TED**  It's the end of July.

**JACKIE**  My calendar is missing—my date book—my—my planner. When did I come to your house?

**TED**  Last week.

**JACKIE**  And I brought a bottle.

**TED**  Johnny Walker.

**JACKIE**  (*beat*)  You have a nice house. We've hardly moved into ours and yours is homey. It has rugs. And furniture and keepsakes.

**TED**  You said you were comfortable.

**JACKIE**  You have a hutch. I always wanted a hutch.

*Joyce can be seen in the kitchen, listening to their conversation.*

**JACKIE**  (*cont.*)  Things smell nice in your house. Food. Meals have been cooked there. We were never home to cook.

**TED**  I try to cook.

**JACKIE**  Where were we? Places. We have photos. Stored in boxes in the basement. Arranged by category. "Travel." "Child." "Miscellaneous." (*beat*) The smell of a pipe. When I came in.

**TED**  I like a pipe on occasion.

**JACKIE**   My father smoked one.

**TED**   You mentioned.

**JACKIE**   He left too. Just before Pam. A, you know, coronary. A heart thing.

**TED**   People leave.

**JACKIE**   I'm supposed to be working . . . on a speech . . . but Ted . . . ?

**TED**   What Jackie?

**JACKIE**   How can the baby live in a world where everyone leaves?

*Ted puts his hand on Jackie's shoulder. Jackie clasps it. Eventually the two embrace, and pull apart only to kiss each other.*

**JACKIE**   Maybe some help with the baby would be good.

**TED**   I sat for my sisters.

**JACKIE**   You mentioned. And so you've had experience. Which is good.

**TED**   And I work out of my house and you come home at night.

**JACKIE**   And we could try this as a temporary arrangement.

**TED**   First thing tomorrow. If you want.

**JACKIE**   As something we'd try.

**TED**   You'll see, Jackie.

*Ted goes off, down the drive. Jackie sits in the lawn chair, struggling against sleep. But, after a moment, he loses the struggle and passes out. Joyce emerges from the house and moves to the drive. She takes out her mini-recorder and speaks into it.*

228

**JOYCE**   Notes for holiday letter, almost August. Jackie claims he is no longer narcoleptic. Perhaps, like me, he is just simply tired.

*She turns off her recorder and makes her way down the drive, and off. After a moment, the door in the fence opens. Once again Pam enters through it. As Jackie sleeps, Pam takes the baby out of the bassinet. She is deciding what she'll do next when she hears someone in the kitchen. Quickly she returns through the fence, taking the baby, closing the door behind her. A moment passes and then Ben appears from the house, wearing a bathrobe of Jackie's.*

**BEN**   I passed out in the shower.

*Jackie wakes.*

**BEN** (*cont.*)   Is it okay if I borrow this robe? This one that says "His" in a monogram? (*Ben looks in the bassinet.*) Who's got the baby?

*Jackie looks in the bassinet.*

**JACKIE**   Where is she? Where is she?!

*Jackie runs down the drive. Ben runs into the house. Mrs. Barnes's flashlight washes over the area. Joyce returns on the drive, calls the police and goes into the house. Ted returns on the drive and looks into the bassinet. Ben comes from the house with a six-pack. He and Ted drink and wait, until Ben passes out against the fence. Soon after, Jackie returns on the drive. It is almost dawn. Joyce comes from the house to hear what news there may be.*

**JACKIE**   Nothing yet.

**JOYCE**   I would've driven you.

**JACKIE**   Nothing.

**JOYCE**  I would've, Jackie. Narcoleptics shouldn't drive. (*beat*) Pam's taken her?

**JACKIE**  That's the thinking.

**TED**  Everyone's been called.

**JACKIE**  I just closed my eyes.

**JOYCE**  I knocked on doors. Up and down the block.

**JACKIE**  How could I have closed my eyes?

**JOYCE**  Incompetence. (*beat*) I've been drinking.

*Ben wakes in the grass.*

**BEN**  What?

**JACKIE**  Someone should take him home.

**TED**  He's okay there.

**BEN**  What is it?

**JOYCE**  Are you okay there? In the grass?

**BEN**  Where is she?

**TED**  There's nothing yet.

**BEN**  Why not? Well, why not?

**JACKIE**  He should go home.

**BEN**  Why should I go home? I'm so much younger than you are! Old people shouldn't tell young people to go home! I'm a young person!

**JACKIE**  The neighbors.

**BEN**  With energy! And—and—

**JOYCE**  He's been drinking.

**BEN**   —and I love Pam! I'm a young person with energy who loves Pam! That should be taken into account when old people say go home! That—should—be— (*He vomits into one of his paint buckets.*) I'm sorry! I'm so sorry!

*Ted helps Ben into the house. A siren is heard approaching Mrs. Barnes's house.*

**JACKIE**   We shouldn't be out here. People will think something's—neighbors will think—they talk and—and will be talking anyway, saying all kinds of God knows what, and if there's a fight, a custody fight—

**JOYCE**   It's okay if you and Ted were involved, Jackie. If I'm living here, what's the sense in pretending? I have friends, even, who are in several male couples. And one female couple. Even I have thought things. Even old Joyce. Older people think things at their "little get-togethers." (*beat*) I thought that was funny.

*It is clear to Jackie that she has continued drinking.*

**JACKIE**   You don't live here.

**JOYCE**   There are all kinds of marriages today, with things so crazy. Steps and halfs. Holidays crazy. Look at our family.

**JACKIE**   We are not related.

**JOYCE**   People darting everywhere. What happened to homesteads? I've been thinking of the relationship between beer and broken homes. And the holidays.

*There is more commotion at Mrs. Barnes's as people congregate there and paramedics are heard radioing a hospital.*

**JACKIE**   We shouldn't be out here!

*Jackie tries to get her inside.*

**JOYCE**  Everybody has to drive to too many houses. Trying to see everyone they're related to who doesn't live with them anymore due to assorted choices. In the days where there was one family, intact, you knew what house you were driving to. And there you stayed. At the homestead. Where you drank. But stayed stationary. Which is why now there are so many drunk drivers at the holidays. Drunk family members trying to prove to their extended broken families that everyone's important! And it's not true!

**JACKIE**  OK.

**JOYCE**  It's not fucking true! I'm cursing all the time now. Young people. Of course we're related.

**JACKIE**  OK!

**JOYCE**  Of course we are!

**JACKIE**  You don't live here.

**JOYCE**  In Westerns there were homesteads.

**JACKIE**  You are my father's wife.

**JOYCE**  People's fathers' wives are related!

**JACKIE**  We are not related!

**JOYCE**  People's fathers' wives are related! In some people's eyes they are! In some cultures! In some ancient—some—

*Pam reenters the yard with the baby. A moment passes and then Joyce goes into the house.*

**JACKIE**  I've written you a letter.

*He picks up his and Joyce's identical mini-recorders.*

**JACKIE** *(cont.)*   It's on one of these. It says things—things—things I can only say when I'm alone. I haven't transcribed it yet.

*Pam goes to hand Jackie the baby, but he steps back from taking her. So Pam returns the baby to the bassinet. And then she is not sure if she will stay or go. She decides to stay, but there is a long silence before either knows how to begin.*

**PAM**   I don't know what I've done. *(beat)* I went to the store. I picked up the things I needed to pick up.

**JACKIE**   You were at the store?

**PAM**   I was in the parking lot. The Grand Union.

**JACKIE**   Last Wednesday. The Grand Union.

**PAM**   The one by the firehouse.

*She doesn't know how to continue.*

**JACKIE**   Wednesday. Last Wednesday.

**PAM**   I couldn't wait till Friday. We were out of so much. The pantry, above the cabinets, the upstairs closet, down to the very last. Floss, paper towels, staples. All kinds of necessary items and I was—I was—

**JACKIE**   Details aren't important.

**PAM**   I was a little upset. At the sink. I was upset a little. Making the list in my head.

**JACKIE**   It's okay.

**PAM**   We were out of so much. And then I had the list. But only in my head. And I was—you write yours down, write everything down—but I try to hold lists in my head. You don't have to decide everything then. *(beat)* And I did get almost everything, but in the parking lot I remembered I forgot cereal.

**JACKIE**  It's okay.

**PAM**  The cereal you like. So I had to go back. But I'd unloaded everything into the car already. And I kept thinking if I go back to the store, will someone steal the groceries? Because I always have this thought that there's someone hiding between all those cars. Teenagers or vagrants. Homeless, hungry people crouching so we can't see them. And I thought, should I risk the groceries I'd already bought for the cereal you like that I forgot? Because I think about decisions lately. (*beat*) And the blacktop was so hot and I worried about the dairy, turning, if I went back. The milk, the ice cream, the margarine, the eggs. If those things sit too long—and I think I was thinking all this and inside the store something happened. In my head, from thinking all this. Keeping it. Instead of writing it down. Something. In the line to pay for the cereal.

**JACKIE**  Pam.

**PAM**  They can tell prices from codes. Black lines that are codes. They can tell what things cost. In the checkout, they tell you what things cost. Groceries are just food but they cost so much. And money's tight now, so you have to decide according to budget, right? And all my groceries were in the car. Hopefully. Details are important, Jackie!

**JACKIE**  Come in the house.

**PAM**  And I knew you were here! Jackie was here with the baby so there was someone, I remember thinking, if I didn't come home. If what was happening in my head didn't stop and—and—if I drove off with the groceries and lived at a motel or something.

**JACKIE**   But you didn't.

**PAM**   Those motel windows everyone can see into. All your private business. The things you're ashamed of—of thinking. I don't know what I've done.

**JACKIE**   This never happened.

**PAM**   Did you get the high chair? Did U.P.S. come?

**JACKIE**   Something was signed for.

**PAM**   It doesn't come assembled. I came with a screwdriver in my bag.

**JACKIE**   This never happened.

**PAM**   Crazy people keep screwdrivers in their bags.

**JACKIE**   You didn't drive off.

**PAM**   Something's wrong. After all that. Something is. The doctors. The effort.

**JACKIE**   Nothing's wrong.

**PAM**   Some women need help from doctors. After everything. The wedding. The house. A family in a house. The money. My trouble conceiving. The doctor, his little talk.

**JACKIE**   You don't need to think of that.

**PAM**   He said we were young people with hope. He said all treasures are guarded by dragons. What crap. Dragons don't have to guard anything. They're imaginary. (*beat*) I feel old. He said we were young.

**JACKIE**   Come inside.

**PAM**   Something has happened, Jackie.

**JACKIE**   Nothing's wrong.

*Pam goes to the baby.*

**PAM**   Isn't she good? Sleeping through everything.

**JACKIE**   She's beautiful.

**PAM**   She scares me. The way she looks at me.

**JACKIE**   She can hardly see.

**PAM**   I want to come home.

*Jackie takes her hand. A moment passes.*

**PAM** (*cont.*)   I don't want to be the mother. (*beat*) I want to come home and I don't want to be the mother. (*beat*) I ordered the high chair because she'll be ready for it soon. It should've come today. U.P.S.

*Another silence.*

**PAM** (*cont.*)   Please, I don't want to be the mother.

**JACKIE**   What is it?

**PAM**   I need to be forgiven.

**JACKIE**   Of course!

**PAM**   I need to be forgiven—and I need to be home. I need to be your wife. I miss affection, and things we did together. And sex. Your smell. Someone else can be the mother.

**JACKIE**   Who?

**PAM**   I'll go back to Mrs. Barnes's house if I have to be the mother.

**JACKIE** (*beat*)   This whole time you've been at Mrs. Barnes's?

236

**PAM**   We've all wanted to see what we look like from the neighbor's house. (*beat*) At night I'd find her places. The attic, the yard, under the stairs by her telephone table. Sitting, pointing a flashlight at the phone. That's how mothers end up. Children scattered.

**JACKIE**   No.

**PAM**   State to state.

**JACKIE**   I promise.

**PAM**   Flashlights and insomnia. Will you be the mother, Jackie? And can I come home? I will be a woman who lives with you. And I will help out. Jackie?

*Ted comes from the house. There is a moment when no one knows what to say.*

**TED**   He's sleeping now. He'll sleep it off.

**JACKIE**   They took Mrs. Barnes to the hospital.

**TED**   That's what that was.

**JACKIE**   Pam was there. Helping out. Now she's home.

*A moment passes.*

**TED**   I should run over and make sure her doors are locked. People find out people are in the hospital and houses get robbed.

**PAM**   Thank you.

*Ted goes through the fence to Mrs. Barnes's house.*

**PAM** (*cont.*)   That's helpful of Ted. He's helpful.

**JACKIE**   Yes.

**PAM**   I could see everyone from there.

**JACKIE**   Could you?

**PAM**   I watched from an upstairs window.

**JACKIE**   Of course.

**PAM**   Maybe you need to be forgiven too, Jackie.

**JACKIE**   (*beat*) You could see—

**PAM**   I could see this whole row of houses.

**JACKIE**   Huh.

**PAM**   The backs of them. Ours. Ted's. Into the windows. Maybe, Jackie, you need to be forgiven, too.

*A silence.*

**JACKIE**   I do.

**PAM**   You need to be forgiven, too.

**JACKIE**   I do.

**PAM**   I do.

*He holds her face and kisses her. He unbuttons her blouse and moves his mouth to her breast and kisses her there.*

**PAM** (*cont.*)   I think anyone could forgive anything they saw from an old lady's window.

*Jackie pulls away and takes her hand.*

**JACKIE**   Come inside. You don't have to be the mother. We'll figure things out and—

*Ted returns through the fence.*

**TED**   Someone locked everything, so it's okay. (*Ted starts to leave.*)

**JACKIE**  Thanks for your offer. Of help with the baby.

**TED**  You're welcome.

**JACKIE**  I bet you were a great sitter for your sisters.

**TED**  I was pretty good, yeah. (*beat*) That's it, Jackie? That's it?

*Joyce enters from the house with her shoulder bag.*

**JOYCE**  Everyone's here.

**JACKIE**  She's home. She's come home with the baby. She was only nearby. And everything can go back. And we'll figure things out—how—how things go. Be more—be more—loose about things. And you can visit—whenever, weekends, and—we can talk about the holidays, who's where. Margy's or yours or somewhere.

**JOYCE**  Everything's in the dryer. I should get on the road.

**TED**  I'll walk you to your car.

**JOYCE**  Thank you. (*beat*) Thank you.

*Ted and Joyce start to go.*

**JACKIE** (*to Joyce*)  People say things. The heat of the moment. We're related, after all.

**JOYCE** (*beat*)  We'll talk about the holidays when we get closer to them. There's no sense in speculating this far off.

*Joyce and Ted once again start down the drive.*

**PAM** (*to Joyce*)  Please stay.

**JACKIE**  Yes, you shouldn't drive this late. Or I can drive your car and take a bus back. That shouldn't take—

**PAM**  No.

**TED**   I can take her.

**JACKIE**   Or Ted could take you.

**PAM**   No. Stay here. With us.

**JACKIE**   Here?

**PAM**   For a while.

**JACKIE**   Stay here? Where here?

**PAM**   Mrs. Barnes has a room.

**JACKIE**   Wait. Wait. So you don't want to be the mother and you want to invite people to stay? Stay for what?

**PAM**   I'd like that, Jackie. I would.

*Jackie doesn't respond.*

**TED**   It's late and I should get home.

**PAM**   And maybe Ted could be our friend.

**JACKIE**   And maybe Ted could be our friend? And what, stay too? Stay where, in the pantry? (*beat*) No, please, wait— what? Ted in the basement? By the washer-dryer? Where should we put Ted? In our room? In the middle of the bed? Unless you won't be there.

**PAM**   Not right away.

**JACKIE**   Oh, so where will you be, or did I miss that? Did I miss where you'll be? At another neighbor's? Looking for another window to sit in? You should tell them now, THEY'RE ALL LISTENING! Where will you be staying?

**PAM**   At first—

**JACKIE**   Where?

**PAM**  Please don't shout.

**JACKIE**  You tell me!

**PAM**  At first in another room. For a time.

**JACKIE**  What other room? What room?

*Ben comes from the house, wrapped in a sheet.*

**BEN**  Pam.

**JACKIE**  Please. Please. I thought I was forgiven?

**PAM**  You are.

**BEN**  Pam.

**JACKIE**  I don't think I am!

**BEN**  Pam, I just wanted to tell you the baseboards are dry. In time for your return.

**PAM**  Thank you.

**JACKIE**  When did you think all this? When did you?

**BEN**  Leave her alone.

**JACKIE**  Excuse me——?

**JOYCE**  Will someone call Mrs. Barnes's children? Or maybe we should discuss this tomorrow?

**JACKIE**  Wait, wait. Call her children for what? What?

**PAM**  She'll need help when she comes home. And she was good to me.

**JOYCE**  And there's a room?

**PAM**  It looks out on this yard.

**JACKIE**  Okay, no one's calling anyone's children!

**PAM**  And Ted can do her shrubs, Jackie. They're overgrown.

**TED**  I'll do it first thing.

**JACKIE**  Okay, wait.

**PAM**  And her banisters are rickety.

**BEN**  I could fix them.

**JACKIE**  Wait—halt—

**PAM**  And we can't stop painting in the middle of this fence—

**JACKIE**  Wait a fucking minute!

**PAM**  It's late, Jackie. We should turn in.

**JACKIE**  But turn in for what?

**BEN**  It's almost morning.

**JACKIE**  Turn in where?

**TED**  It's becoming light.

**JOYCE**  The baby will be up soon.

**JACKIE**  But who turns in where? We should—we should—what? Chart it out—in our heads, at least. Is Ben between me and Ted and you? Is that what this is about? Will you tell me?

**PAM**  No, Jackie.

**TED**  Can I hold the baby? Before I go?

**JACKIE**  Will somebody please tell me?

*Pam lifts the baby from the bassinet and hands her to Ted.*

**BEN**  We're tired, Jackie.

**JACKIE**  Don't call me Jackie—why are you calling me Jackie? And telling me what to do? Who is this little shit?

**PAM**  Stop it, Jackie.

**JOYCE**  People are sleeping. We should be sleeping.

**BEN**  I'm not a little shit.

**PAM**  It can wait.

**JACKIE**  No one is sleeping!

**JOYCE**  You'll feel better later.

**JACKIE**  Don't tell me how I'll feel! You are here by the good graces of someone—

**PAM**  Stop this.

*Joyce moves to Ted.*

**JOYCE**  I'll take her.

*Ted hands Joyce the child.*

**JACKIE**  She isn't everybody's baby! She doesn't need all this handling!

**PAM**  Please, Jackie.

**JACKIE**  She shouldn't be passed around like she's—

**PAM**  Stop this!

**JACKIE**  —like nuts at Christmas! She's mine! And I'll—okay, if you can't be the mother—she's no one else's—no one here. She's not yours then, she's mine! You abdicated.

**PAM**  No.

**JACKIE**  I'M TELLING YOU WHAT'S WHAT! It won't be all—this MESS!

**PAM**   I didn't, Jackie.

**JACKIE**   Go inside, Pam. Go inside.

**PAM**   I didn't!

**JACKIE**   Go inside. And EVERYBODY go!

**PAM**   I don't want them to go.

**JACKIE**   Everybody go, please.

**PAM**   We need help, Jackie.

**JACKIE**   EVERYBODY PLEASE GO!

**PAM**   I don't want anyone going!

**BEN**   And I'm not a little shit. I have what she needs. And you better get some. Or I'm in and you're out. I know it.

*Jackie ignores this and starts to clean the mess in the yard.*

**JACKIE**   She abdicated and I'm not the one who's out—*(to Ben)* YOU'RE out! *(to the others)* And YOU and YOU. Everyone's out but ME and I have everything here to do this myself! I have towels and—and clean diapers. Schedule of times. Feedings, naps. Not now. Later. Soon.

**PAM**   We should go in, Jackie.

**JACKIE**   Police, feedings, naps—diapers, poison, fire.

**PAM**   It's morning, Jackie.

**JACKIE**   Brightly colored keys, books. This is the whole world I need, right here. Pick her up! Make faces! Keep her clean! Anything else?

**PAM**   That's all, Jackie.

**JACKIE**   I'm forgetting anything—there's a list—

**PAM**  That's everything.

**JACKIE**  —there's books we've read and—she's to—

**PAM**  For now, it is.

**JACKIE**  —she should—interact with others!

**JOYCE**  Go on, Jackie.

**JACKIE**  When possible.

**JOYCE**  I'll follow with the baby.

**JACKIE**  In the books they recommend it. (*Scrambling in the grass, Jackie finds both his and Joyce's mini-recorders.*) Whose is this? WHOSE IS WHOSE? (*Jackie turns on one recorder and his father's voice issues forth.*)

**JACKIE SENIOR'S VOICE**  Notes for my son, on the occasion of his becoming a father. Notes . . . notes . . .

*But Jackie Senior's voice has been taped over by Jackie Junior's . . .*

**JACKIE'S VOICE**  Notes for Dad's service. Mention clubs and organizations, hobbies in later years: origami, football pool—

*Jackie turns it off. He then fast-forwards through the tape—but everywhere he lands on the tape, he hears his own voice.*

**JACKIE**  I never changed the tape it came with. I assumed it was blank.

**JOYCE**  I put a note on it.

**JACKIE**  I didn't read it.

*Jackie throws his father's recorder in the grass.*

**JOYCE**  I should go over your speech in the next few days. (*beat*) Just a few words.

**JACKIE**  I can't write a speech about someone who told me nothing! About things I needed to know—and—and—and—and—and—and—

*Joyce hands Jackie his child. He holds her silently for a moment.*

**JACKIE** *(cont.)*  Do you think all this handling is good for her? *(He puts her against his shoulder, so her ear is close to his mouth. He speaks to his child.)* This isn't usually what goes on. It won't be like this when you're older. Things will have sorted out. You'll come to think of us as the ones who didn't know. You'll forsake us as—as the ones who—who didn't know. And we won't blame you. You'll be right. No one from the past will blame you for leaving them behind. As you move ahead. As you replace us. In the scheme of things. As people leave. And—and—and—some return. Thankfully. As the world becomes better. Everything is about to be and very little now matters. But everything soon will. And you are that. You are all that! And what this is, is an extraordinary time. *(beat)* Please. *(beat)* Please!

*The sun is now up. Jackie is about to take the baby into the house, but he stops.*

**JACKIE** *(cont.)*  I will be the father. And mother when I can be. When I cannot we will disperse the responsibility. *(to pam)* You will be the wife. I will be your husband. Ted can be a neighbor who helps outside. Ben will keep the house in shape. Joyce will take care of Mrs. Barnes. Margueretta remains the baby. Until we decide differently. Is everything, for now, in order?

*They all look at one another and then decide.*

**PAM**  Yes.

**TED**  Yes.

**BEN** Yes.

**JOYCE** Yes.

**JACKIE** Yes.

*Satisfied, Jackie heads for the house with the baby. But he only makes it a step or two before the sprinklers go on, shooting up around the perimeter of the yard. They all watch the water a moment as the sun gets very high in the sky, making the water brighter and brighter.*

*End of Play.*